DIARY OF A NIGI

PILOT

1939 – 1945

by

SQUADRON LEADER

DOUGLAS GREAVES DFC and BAR

Published by Suzanne Marshall
Text copyright © 2016 Suzanne Marshall

Suzanne Marshall has asserted her right under the Copyright, Designs and Patents Act 1988 to be identified as the publisher of this work.

Acknowledgements

The cover picture is a reproduction of an oil painting by the author, Douglas Greaves.

Thanks to Phil Watson for all his work in publishing this diary.

FOREWORD

Written in his own hand from the day he signed up in October 1939 as a trainee pilot to the day he was 'demobbed' in October 1945, this poignant and often riveting diary by Squadron Leader Douglas Greaves D.F.C and Bar, records, in typical understated RAF style, the minutiae of everyday life in the services, as well as the horror he and his comrades endured and the heroism they all displayed.

Subsequently 'typed up' by his own father, Wilfred, the manuscript was treasured for many years by his wife Marion and all of us, his children: Cameron Greaves, Yvette Drabble and Suzanne Marshall.

Suzanne, herself a writer re-typed the diary on to a computer, and Cameron, living in Australia, later produced a small number of books for the family.

However, our mother expressed a wish before she died for the diary to be published more widely as both an e-book and a printed book.

At pains not to interfere with our father's admirable style, we have resisted the temptation to correct occasional inconsistencies relating to punctuation, abbreviations, and the use/non-use of military time.

Primarily we wish it to be enjoyed and remembered in honour of all the valiant men of 255 and 25 squadron, both those who survived and those who lost their lives.

Yvette Drabble
Cameron Greaves
Suzanne Marshall

DIARY OF A NIGHT FIGHTER PILOT

by

DOUGLAS GREAVES

It is **October 15th 1939**. The war has been in progress for about six weeks and I have been married since the day it was declared. This has been a happy period for me personally, in fact so much so that I have not given much serious thought as to how the future will affect us. Germany has practically completed the invasion of Poland with the assistance of Russia but apart from a few minor frontier incidents, a spectacular air raid on Kiel Canal, and quite a number of our merchant ships being sunk by German 'U' boats, neither England nor France have been involved in any major engagements.

So apart from the blackout restrictions, a noticeable presence of gas masks and a slackening in trade, the fact that there is a war on is not having the disastrous effects that I expected. Prior to this, I had always imagined that in the case of a conflict with Germany our people would be faced with almost nightly destruction from the gigantic German air armada.

Although up to this date I have been able to view the situation somewhat as an outsider, I am now becoming aware that before long it will be very much my business and that whatever I do I am bound to become involved. It certainly is a distasteful thought, not just from the point of view of possible self-destruction, but because it means that sooner or later I will have to leave Marie, close up the house, and scrap all the plans I have for our future for an indefinite period. It will also undoubtedly be a blow for her to have to leave our home and for us to be separated so quickly.

There is also the Works to consider. Father was finding it a big strain before the war and the position is considerably more worrying now. Up to the present my efforts have been helping him in the struggle and I don't relish the idea of leaving when I could be of most use, particularly as I know he has been making this effort chiefly for my benefit.

These thoughts become more prominent in my mind every day but I am fully aware that it is only a question of time before my turn comes and I must consider which part of this great war machine I am going to become involved in when it does.

I know that to wait for conscription inevitably means the infantry and I should like to avoid that at all costs. Most of my friends have joined anti-aircraft units but there are now definitely no more vacancies left in that direction. I certainly feel that if I have to be in it, I will go for some job that I have an interest in and also feel that the Air is the only place in which I can genuinely claim this. I have always had a fascination for aircraft. During the last two years I have flown privately to the extent of about thirty hours and recently became a member of the Civil Air Guard, accounting for another fifteen. Yes, this is the section I must apply for but I don't want to go before my time if I can help it.

The chance has just presented itself. I have received a letter from the Civil Air Guard giving me the opportunity of going before the RAF selection committee with a view to entering the service for training as a pilot. The main point of interest is that it also states, that in the event of my being selected, I should be sworn in, fitted out with uniform and sent home on indefinite leave for a period of three to four months. This is just the type of proposition I have been waiting for because it means I can enter for the job most suited to me and, at the same time, I should not be called for service before the date that I would otherwise be conscripted. It would also offer me a good chance of promotion and if I am going to be in the service for a few years that point is certainly a consideration.

I have shown Marie the letter and explained to her what I propose doing. I think she has realised lately that I shall be compelled to join something sooner or later and I therefore hope that my suggestion did not come as too much of a surprise although I must say I feel pretty rotten having to tell her so quickly.

The next thing is to discuss it with father. He understands the difficulties I am up against as well as I do and shares my opinion that the chances of exemption are very thin. He is not very keen on the idea of me going in the Air Force although he agrees that it is better than the infantry. At the conclusion of our conversation he turned to me and said,

"Well, Doug, I will leave it to you to do what you think is best and if you go I will try to keep the works going for you until you come back."

The last sentence gives me a lump in the throat. Poor Dad. As far back as my earliest memories he has always worked so very hard with the factories and, just when he needs me most, I have to leave him. It does not seem to be playing the game but what can I do?

The letter from the Civil Air Guard states that, if I am interested, I should go down to the Leeds recruitment centre on the 20th for an interview. During the day, whilst driving through the town, I bump into Henry Heaton who tells me that he has received a similar letter and intends to go to the interview on the 20th too. We agree that we shall meet and go down together. I am pleased that I have met someone else who is going on the same day and, if we are successful, hope it will be possible for us to keep together when we are called up.

Today is 20th October. Marie comes down to the works in the car with me. I arranged to meet Henry at 10.00 am for the interview at 10.30 so I have just time to call at the works for half an hour. Afterwards Marie runs me round to the Heatons and drops Henry and I at the Recruitment Centre.

I don't know quite what to expect here. There are dozens of fellows waiting and I should imagine that they are applying to enter the army. Most of them seem to be getting sent away and are told that there are no vacancies yet and that they will have to wait until they are conscripted. After waiting for a few minutes, we decide to walk up to the officious looking sergeant sitting behind a desk full of papers. He is too busy to take any notice of us but when we bluntly make our presence known, he condescends to look up and in a sort of growl enquires what we want. I thump my letter from the Civil Air Guard down in front of him and Henry does likewise. After impatiently glancing through

4

them, he indicates that we should go up to the third floor where the RAF section is dealt with.

We have now walked up three flights of stairs, where we find another group of fellows waiting and a corporal at the door instructs us to take our place in the queue. After half an hour we eventually arrive at a desk where a second sergeant is seated. We again show our letters and he furnishes us both with two long forms to be filled in and tells us to sit down and enter name and address, next of kin, occupation and dozens of questions which appear to have no bearing on the matter. After handing these in, we are sent to the next floor and told to report to yet another sergeant. This involves another long wait and eventually the answering of many more questions. Satisfied at last, the sergeant gives us both a chit, telling us to report back in the afternoon for a preliminary Medical exam. We are feeling pleased to get out of the place for a while and go into the town for some lunch.

Afterwards we again report to the recruiting centre and once again we are obliged to wait in a queue for the Medical examiners. When my turn comes I am told to fully strip and am sent into a room screened off into about eight sections. There are examiners in each section and each one specialises in a different portion of the body. I go into the first cubicle which is for eyes, the second is for ears, then lungs, height, weight and so on. Finally I am told to go and dress and am sent into the chief examiner's office. He reads the form that has all the reports on it and writes out a small chit saying that I am A1.

I am now sent down to the third floor again and am told to wait for the Commanding Officer. Henry is also waiting, having also passed the medical A1. There is a small party of us now apparently all applicants for Air Crew. We wait for an hour, after which an airman announces that the C.O. will see us. We are led into his office and line up in front of his desk. He informs us that we have to report back again at 10.30 am on the 23rd when we shall be sent to Cardington to appear before the Selection Board. I go down to the works as usual on the 23rd complete with gas mask, toothbrush, razor and mackintosh and meet Henry as arranged. We walk down to the recruiting centre.

Outside the entrance, we meet a friend of Henry's who is also going to Cardington for the interview. I am introduced to Alex Lane. We all three walk into the room where we had been told to report and sit down to wait for the C.O. After a while we are again shown into his office and he informs us that we shall be catching the 11.30 am train. He gives us a few hints on going before the selection committee and tells us that they are rather severe on Air Crew lately. He also tells us that a high knowledge of Mathematics and Trigonometry is required. This remark rather shakes my confidence because it is several years since I touched Trig or Maths and my knowledge certainly cannot be considered high. He also reminds us that we shall be having another medical exam which will be very detailed. After he has finished his comments, he gives Henry an envelope containing our details and a shilling each.

There are about nine of us going down together - two fellows from York Civil Air Guard as pilots and several others from Yeadon C.A.G. We catch the train at 11.30 am. Everybody seems very pessimistic about the chances of getting in and we hear stories about only three out of the last ten that went down being successful.

The journey eventually develops into a game of Pontoon. It is eight o'clock before we arrive in the station at

Bedford and we find that there are about twenty other fellows from various other centres in Yorkshire waiting there. Nobody seems to have any idea what we are to do and there is nobody to meet us in so I ring up Cardington from a call box. They say they are sending some transport down. After half an hour, a large open vehicle arrives and we all clamber in the back. It rather reminds me of a cattle truck. The journey from Bedford to Cardington is unpleasant and it is now raining hard and very cold. The position of the Camp is made conspicuous by the large Air Ship hangars which once housed the airships R100 and R101. These are now used as a Balloon Training unit and consequently there are apparently no air-craft here at all.

We are met by the dismal sight of hundreds of Army huts when we dismount from the lorry. It would be pretty terrible to be stationed in a place like this but I suppose we shall only be here for a day at the outside.

A red faced corporal with a rough Scots accent addresses us in a very dictatorial manner which nearly tempts me to inform him that we are not in the services yet but my better judgment checks me.

He takes our names and Henry's envelope and then marches us across the camp, until we come to what is apparently known as "C" Flight. Here we are met by a flight sergeant, a man with a very broad southern accent and a lot of decayed teeth which causes a spray to come from his mouth when he talks. He takes us to the store hut and issues us with a towel, knife, fork, spoon and mug. I shall always remember his remark when issuing the latter articles.

"Now 'ere's a mag and don't you come to me and say you 'aven't 'ad one cause you 'ave, see, and if you lose it, it'll caust yer a tanner."

We are now shown to our hut where we can leave our few belongings. It is a cold place with rows of iron beds with biscuits (the name they call the small mattresses) and blankets stacked up on them. The place looks very damp. I am sure it has not been used for weeks. The red faced Corporal now tells us to take our eating appliances and go for some supper. We are marched to the canteen, which is a larger hut full of trestle tables and forms. There are queues of Airmen along the side of the hut waiting to collect their food and fill their mugs with tea. Having waited our turn, we find a table which is crammed with more people than it can hold to give sufficient elbow room. The meal consists of two sausages. I put my knife in one of them. It is so hard that it cracks. It is the most revolting thing I have ever tasted. Henry and Alex and several of the other people from our hut seem to have arrived at the same conclusion so we decide to leave the eating part for the time being. We go back to the hut and learn that we can go into the "NAAFI" for a drink and can also get food there. We gladly jump at the idea. The vicinity of the "NAAFI" is soon indicated by the strains of a heavily played piano and the jarring voices of some singing airmen. We order beers and some food which is a slight improvement on the Canteen.

A very bored looking airman at the counter tells us of how he has been at Cardington for four months waiting for a posting as a flight mechanic. He says he has never heard of pilots and observers being sent down here before.

By this time I am getting to know quite a few of the people who came down from Yorkshire as prospective air crew. There is Joe Holmes from Normanton, a fellow called Pope who used to be at Giggleswick College with Leslie Batty, apparently nick-named Pip, John Decker from Carlisle and a tall ginger haired fellow from Halifax, Joe Stott.

At 9.30 pm we decide to go back to our hut. It is still raining and very cold. I arrange my bed and get into it inwardly cursing for not bringing any pyjamas. It is certainly the most uncomfortable night I have ever spent in my life. In the first place, the bed is damp and the biscuits are very hard compared to the soft mattress that I have been used to and secondly, I had not realised that there is a special way of making these little beds.

At last the night is over. I have not closed my eyes once and my opinion of the RAF has altered quite a lot in the last twenty four hours. We are called at six o'clock by the corporal and it is still completely dark but for the first time in my life I don't think it is too early to get up.

We all get dressed and I am pleased to learn that everybody else has also had a sleepless night. We pack our beds up and are marched down to breakfast. I take rather a pale view of being marched about as we are not really in the RAF yet and this indignant little corporal puts me in a bad temper.

We have more queuing for breakfast and more distasteful food to try and eat. The menu here seems to consist only of sausages. This ordeal over, we go and wait in our huts again and are then marched to the other end of the camp to wait for the selection committee.

An officer finally turns up and gives us some more disheartening news about the qualities required by the

9

selection committee for pilots and observers. He encourages people who are not extremely hot at Maths and Trigonometry to apply as Air gunners. It is extraordinary how many are influenced by him, scrap all their ambitions to be a pilots on the spot and go in as Air gunners. Although after this I feel that my chances of getting in are absolutely nil, I am determined that I shall be a pilot or nothing, so I fill in more forms and continue to wait.

About two hours have passed and the door that we have all been watching opens again. A rather more pleasant than usual corporal appears and calls out Heaton. I whisper good luck to him and Henry goes in. This door has opened about seven times before with similar announcements and nervous people have gone in but we have not seen anybody come out yet which is rather disturbing because we cannot determine how many have been accepted and what the ordeal is like.

Finally the deciding moment comes and my name is called. The corporal shows me in and I walk forward instinctively coming to attention in front of a desk behind which is seated an Air Vice Marshall and a civilian. He is the man that fires the mathematical questions. It is surprising that although I am not yet in the services, the sight of the bands on the Air Vice Marshall's sleeve have quite a disturbing effect on me. He asks me to sit down however and the gesture puts me at my ease.

"Well Greaves, I see that you want to be a pilot. Dangerous job you know!" I answer that I understand that, inwardly thinking that it cannot be worse than the infantry. He then asks me quite a number of very stupid, simple questions, in fact so simple that I suspect a trap somewhere. One was, "What is the difference between rates and income tax?" He is apparently satisfied with my answers and asks the civilian to go ahead. His first question is about how to find the height of a hangar. Fortunately, I know something about Theodalites and am able to give another satisfactory reply. He then asks me a question on Algebra which I am unable to answer, so I tell him that I have not touched it since school. Several others follow. I respond to some but not others. Finally the Air Vice Marshall says, "Alright Greaves, if you are up to the medical standard you will be acceptable for training as a pilot."

The Air Crew medical exam is rather more severe than the one we had in Leeds and takes about two hours. Three quarters of an hour of this time is spent on eyesight and there are several other probable stumbling blocks such as blowing up a mercury tube and holding it there for a minute and a quarter. They also spin me round in a revolving chair and then ask me to stand on one leg after it. I am more than a little surprised when I manage to pass this exam and feel much happier when the corporal shows me into another room where I see some of the applicants again. Apparently these are all the successful ones.

Henry Heaton has got through and also Joe Holmes. Alex Lane was considered too old for a pilot but is accepted as an observer. He is not too pleased about this. Pip Pope, Joe Stott and a small Canadian fellow called Aston are all accepted as pilots under training. John Docker has gone in as an Air Gunner. All the others have been caught out either by the Air Vice Marshall or the medical exam - amongst them two fellows from York.

We now all stand up for a Padre who has just arrived and are sworn in. After this we are all eager to get back home again but our red faced Corporal says he has no instructions to let us go yet. This is rather annoying as no one relishes spending another night like the last one but as it seems impossible to do any more about it, we settle down to some pints of beer in the "NAAFI" and go to bed at 9.30 pm which is the lights out time. I manage to get some instruction from an Old Hand on how to make a bed and, although the night is spent in considerable discomfort, it is quite an improvement on the previous one.

The next morning the routine is the same as before, even to the extent of having the same sausages for breakfast. The day goes on and the corporal still knows nothing of us going home. He is not a very bright type of fellow so we try to make applications to see the Commanding Officer ourselves, only to be reminded that we are Aircraftsmen Second Class (A.C.2's) which is the lowest form of life in the Air Force and that the C.O. is a very busy man. All our efforts to see anyone in authority are unsuccessful and we are obliged to spend a further night at Cardington. We are now all getting very fed up and beginning to wonder when we shall be able to get out of this infernal place. None of us have been able to eat very much so far and we are all looking forward to the chance of getting a good meal.

The next day comes and we are issued with service respirators and given gas lectures. In the afternoon we are all inoculated and vaccinated. I pass out after the inoculation and feel very stupid about it. After this I make another unsuccessful attempt to see the adjutant about going home. I am now beginning to lose all faith in getting there at all and am more and more worried about Marie as she expected me back two days ago. If it did happen that I don't get back, there is the house to consider. Marie would not want to be there on her own and we have only just got the place furnished. There are a thousand things I want to see to in

Leeds and I get more depressed about it every minute. It seems impossible to find out anything in this place.

We go to bed again and next morning my inoculation has taken effect on me. I have a high temperature and feel absolutely rotten mentally and physically. The Corporal gives me permission to stay in bed so I perspire and shiver alternately all day. At night I manage to get up and I am now so hungry that for the first time I manage to eat anything I can get. My stomach has ceased to be touchy about food and is quite capable of tackling anything.

I see Henry and Joe at night and am surprised to see that they are no longer in civvies. Their uniforms look absolutely dreadful. They are a bad fit with dog-collar tunics. I had at least consoled myself with the thought that in the RAF we should be able to wear a collar and tie but these things are much worse than wearing battle dress.

Both Henry and Joe seem to be of the opinion that our chances of getting back now are practically nil so, after a lot of wangling, I manage to get out of camp for half an hour to ring Marie. She is pleased to hear from me again but very upset when I express my doubts about getting home. Dad says he will send me a letter from the works to the commanding officer saying that I have important matters to clear up. This seems the only way of getting anything through to the C.O.

Another night passes and next day I am equipped with uniform. It is an appalling fit and is at least as bad as Henry's. I find the boots and uniform very uncomfortable after my civilian clothes, in fact the tunic is so bad that I re-tailor it to some extent myself.

In my hut there are about twenty people. They are a very mixed selection. Most of them are flight mechanics and people for general duties and there are one or two wireless operators. Henry and Joe are in a different hut. The only other Air crews in this hut are Alex Lane and Pip. The following morning the letter arrives from the works.

The commanding officer calls me in and after a lot of trouble condescends to give me a forty-eight hour pass. I also learn quite officially that we are in the Air Force to stay and will not be sent back on indefinite leave. This confirms my worst suspicions but I realise only too well that I have no say at all in my future actions. I get away after lunch the following day and do not get into Leeds until late at night. I fell very humiliated in my ill-fitting tunic but my great coat is not too bad so I wear this as much as possible.

It is heaven to be with Marie again for a couple of days but the time goes far too quickly. We decide that the only thing to do is to empty our house and let it out for the duration and for Marie to go to Chester until such time as she will be able to live out with me. I talk light heartedly about this but at present the possibility seems out of the question.

The time has come for me to go back again and I am feeling terribly fed up as I move out of the station in the train. I get back to Cardington for supper where I meet Henry, Joe and Alex who say that they have started doing drill and physical training every day now and that it is keeping them very busy.

Next morning I find that they had not exaggerated the position. I am up at 6.00 am, have to shave, clean my boots and buttons, make my bed and polish my floor space before breakfast. I get into breakfast at 7.00 and have to be on the first drill parade at 7.30. This consists of being marched up and down the barrack square - a very tiring business which goes on until 9.0 o'clock when we have ten minutes to change into physical training kit. P.T. goes on until 10.30 when we get a quarter of an hour to slip into the NAAFI for a bun and a cup of coffee. After this we have another session of drill before lunch.

At 1.30, after lunch, we have more drill until 3 o'clock, after that P.T. again, then tea followed by another hour's drill. After this I am so exhausted that I make my bed and fall asleep on it. I have already developed one or two blisters on my feet which are very painful. I am woken up by the corporal after about an hour because I should have been cleaning my webbing equipment.

This routine goes on day after day and somehow I manage to get used to it. After the first week we are allowed out of camp after duty until 9.30 pm, so Henry, Alex, Joe, Pip and myself go down to the local pub whenever possible and drink beer all evening. It is a relief to get out of that infernal place if only for an hour or two. Our duties do not get any less as time goes on because we now find that we have rifle drill as well and also have fatigues to do. These are most unpleasant chores which can be anything from cleaning latrines, serving out sausages, washing plates or cleaning floors. Fortunately I manage to avoid the first option. The extraordinary thing is that nobody seems to have heard of Air crew coming here before and we are certainly all surprised to find ourselves doing rifle drill when we joined up to fly.

This programme continues for about a fortnight and then the C.O. comes to watch us parade. This apparently means that we have passed out and are ready for posting but little did we know at this stage that this depends upon whether the Initial Training Wings can take us rather than when we have completed our rifle drill.

When I was in Leeds on my forty-eight hour pass, I went to my tailor and got him to make me a decent tunic. I have now received this and do not feel so self-conscious going out of camp. We don't in any case get out much because there is not much time between when we finish and 9.30 pm so, apart from our few trips down to the local pub of an evening, we tend to stay in.

There has been an outbreak of German measles on the camp and Henry has caught it. He is very annoyed because he has to stay in sick quarters and to be in quarantine for ten days. He is rather afraid that we shall be posted without him. Even though we are supposed to have passed out, we continue to do drill and fatigues. I have got used to this type of thing now and my feet have become toughened against blisters. My stomach too can now cope with any sort of food.

There is very little to write about the many days that follow. The routine does not vary and it feels as though we shall never leave this place. Marie comes down to stay in Bedford for a few days and I am able to get out to see her on Sunday afternoon and for a few evenings, I am annoyed when trying to get out one night that the corporal details me to go and guard a Fairy Battle that has crashed in a field near the camp. I have to spend the whole night walking round the machine with my rifle.

The weather is freezing now and there are frequent falls of snow. The huts are very cold and it goes against the grain to get up at 6.0 o'clock in a morning and queue outside for our turn to have breakfast in the canteen.

Henry Heaton has come out of sick quarters again and all we air crew are put together in one hut with some other ground crew. This raises my spirits a little because we now have a monopoly of the hut and this develops a mutual camaraderie which smooths over many of the unpleasant things.

At last Christmas has arrived and we are all given seven days leave. I am very excited about this. The thought of being able to spend a whole week with Marie is something I look forward to more than anything on earth. Alex, Joe, Henry, Rip, Joe Stott and myself all live in the same part of the world so we travel up on the same train and get into Leeds late in the evening. The seven days goes much too quickly. Marie and I go to several dances in Harrogate over Christmas but all too soon I find myself having to pack ready to go back again.

Dad lends me the Wolsley and I drive back with Alex, Joe, Henry and Pip. A driver from Cardigan Press takes the car back to Leeds. We are all fed up about going back but within a day the excellent news comes through that we are posted. There is much celebrating this night and we all have more beer than is good for us before we stumble into bed. This is not surprising when you consider that we have spent just over ten weeks at Cardington and I am quite certain that ten weeks in prison could not have been more unpleasant.

CAMBRIDGE NO 1 - INITIAL TRAINING WING

Next morning we all have nasty hangovers but manage somehow to pack all our belongings and get on parade ready to be marched to the train. The train is late as usual and we get into Cambridge at about 3.0 o'clock. We now discover that we are to be billeted in various colleges and unfortunately are to be divided out according to the initial letters of our surnames. I am in the party that is marched to Clare College. Also in the same party are Henry, Joe and Joe Stott. Pip Pope and Aston (usually known as Canader) and Mac are in a party for Trinity Hall College.

Clare is an imposing newly built college and Joe and I share a room together. This is really quite comfortable and is an immense improvement on Cardington. The fellows that are already here are all acting sergeants because they joined the Voluntary Reserves before the war. The college dining room is a very nice old hall and the food is a great improvement on what we have been eating for the last ten weeks. We take it in turns to be Mess Orderlies, whose job it is to serve meals to the other chaps and the system works well.

All the people here are Pilots Under Training and the discipline is very strong. We have a Warrant Officer called Tynan who is the most aggressive, frightening man I have yet to meet in the service. It is more than one's life is worth to be a second late on parade.

Although life is much better, it is still very hard work. We have drill and Physical Training several times a day and on top of this we get lectures on Maths, Navigation, Armament and Morse. So for the first time we feel that we are doing something that is going to be of use to us.

Practically all the colleges in Cambridge are used by the Initial Training Wing and all the trainees can be recognised by the white hands that we wear on our hats. It is a rule that everybody must be in at ten o'clock but on quite a number of the evenings Joe and I stay in and study our Navigation and Maths etc., because shortly we shall be expected to take exams on all the subjects and we are reminded only too often that failure to pass means "Out."

Joe was a school master before the war and so this sort of thing is second nature to him as he has been passing exams all his life. In contrast, I find it a deuce of a strain to get down to it all. The daily routine is now up at 6.30 am and parade at 7.00 am with buttons cleaned. Then we are marched down to the old Clare dining hall for breakfast. We parade again at 7.45 am and a roll call is taken. If anyone is missing, he will be at the mercy of Warrant Officer Tynan. (I was only late on one occasion but the conflict with Tynan was so unpleasant that I was ten minutes early for every subsequent parade at Cambridge.) We are then all marched on to the large grass lawn between Clare and St John's where we form up for an inspection by the Commanding Officer.

Pip, Canader and Mac from Trinity all parade here as well because the two colleges have the same C.O. He is Flight Lieutenant Kelly, a very unpleasant individual at any time of the day but particularly so on his morning inspection. Untidy haircuts, dull buttons, dirty boots, less than perfect shaves etc are major offences to him.

When all this is over, either we stay to be drilled by the ferocious Mr Tynan and the Trinity college people march to Chaucer Road for lectures or vice versa so it means that either the morning is drill and afternoon lectures of morning lectures and afternoon drill.. The period that is allotted to drill is the most unpleasant part as Warrant Officer Tynan shouts and raves the whole time and there are few people in the squad who survive the morning without having a dressing down from him. He tries to get us marching in step and forming twos and fours by repeatedly calling out Um-Pu-Ti-Pa. We cannot understand what this means and nobody dares to ask. Joe Holmes who is fluent in French finally decides that, as he was old enough to have been in the last war, he had probably heard the phrase "un petit peu" meaning "a little bit" in France.

We parade again for lunch and tea and usually finish our day at about 6.0o'clock but as previously mentioned, it is essential to spend a good many evenings studying if we wish to even get to a flying training school.

We hear one day that the senior course (all sergeants) have had their exams and are anxiously awaiting the results. One lunch time when we return from drill, we are rather shaken to see an unhappy bunch of sergeants with their kit bags waiting to be marched away. These, we learn, are the failures - their chances of being pilots have gone for good. They can either leave the service or lose their stripes and remuster for some other job. This doubly emphasises the necessity to study at night and many people who had not hitherto been doing so stop going out and start concentrating on their Navigation. Also, every evening the constant buzz of Morse keys can be heard throughout the college.

One day we are marched to the Initial Training Wing Stores, which are at Jesus college and are issued with our flying clothing. This does a lot to cheer us up and we all feel that the day when we shall move to flying schools is not far away.

We have not had any leave so far and we are very excited one weekend when we are all given a 48 hour pass. Henry Heaton has got his Aston Martin down here so Pip, Joe, myself and Henry all go to Leeds in it. It is a fast motor and Henry makes short work of the journey up the Great North Road. It is a happy feeling to be travelling back to see Marie again at such a speed. 48 hours passes incredibly fast and I barely seem to have said hello to Marie before it is time to kiss her goodbye again. The same beautiful Aston Martin that brought me to her so quickly turns out to be the beast that takes me away again at equal speed.

There is still a lot of snow about in Cambridge and it is very cold. We find it bitter on our drill mornings but whatever the weather Warrant Officer Tynan keeps us at it.

We are now getting along quite well with the various subjects although I am still rather shaky on Maths and have difficulty getting down to Morse. It is a monotonous business and gets on my nerves quickly. I cope better with Navigation and also with Armament. Fortunately, I always had an interest in mechanics and it does not take me long to thoroughly understand the mechanism of both a Browning and Vickers gun. The only way to be sure of getting through the exams is to keep on studying at night and overcome the temptation to pack it up and go out for a drink.

Apart from physical training we have several afternoons a week for sport. I have not played Rugger for years but I play quite a lot of squash. Joe used to be a professional Rugger player for Leeds so he is often off to represent the Initial Training Wing against local teams.

I have not mentioned the war lately because it is at rather a stalemate. The weather has been the worst for ten years in France and so the Army activity has been practically nil. There are still quite a number of our merchant ships being sunk by enemy submarines but our convoy system seems to cut this down to a minimum. The RAF have carried out several raids on factories in Germany but again the weather has kept most of them grounded.

It is now February 1940 and we have been at Cambridge for almost three weeks. We still have to parade for roll call at 7.45 am but are spending more time at Chaucer road to attend classes in Maths, Navigation Signals, Airforce Law, Armaments and Morse code. This entails a half hour march each way. We are no longer exposed to the drilling ordeal by Warrant Officer Tynan but on some days we have to do four hour route marches under a most unpleasant corporal with a voice only slightly less in volume than W.O. Tynan. For these marches we are assembled two abreast forming a long caterpillar which starts off threading its way round the narrow streets of Cambridge. We would often try to get at the back of this line and drop off when the file went round corners and then go to the WYMCA or Salvation Army rooms where Military Police are not supposed to be allowed. It amazed me that the corporal did not seem to notice how much shorter his file was when he returned to Cambridge.

We are now told that we will be required to sit our exams early in March so the swatting up is much more intense. A distraction to this is that we have to do a rota for guard duty on the RA installations near Cambridge. This calls for two patrols walking round in the snow with a shouldered rifle. The date for the exams has now arrived and we have to sit in a large room at separate spaced desks with a strict time limit for the different papers. I did the best I could but it was a very anxious time waiting several days for the results. When they came through I was very pleased to see that I had just scraped by in Maths, done well in Navigation and had a reasonable pass in the other subjects apart from Morse code where I had not made the required speed. Fortunately, I was not alone in this so they decided to let it go.

We all thought that we would now be sent to Elementary Flying Training School of E.F.T.S. as they are called but we still had to endure the marching and physical training until the end of March. Then one morning the Station Commander called us into the large hall at Claire College and said that we would get a week's leave before being asked to report to flying training Schools. He went to great length wishing us good luck and success in our flying service.

I am able to return to Marie again at our new house in Horsforth. She has been living alone during this time but has made friends with Ronald and Joclyn Kellett, a newly married couple living in the house opposite. Unfortunately, she has not been able to use our old Hillman Minx due to severe petrol rationing and it has been locked away in the garage whilst I was away. The winter has been very severe and the exceptional frost cracked the cylinder block. This cannot be repaired so we have had to accept a scrap price for it from a local garage. I have now heard that once we are at flying schools or squadrons we will most probably be able to live out so we both decided that when this could be done we would let the house for a temporary period.

I have returned to Cambridge and am informed that my posting is to Number 56 O.T.U, which is an operational training unit, at Sutton Bridge in Norfolk with one or two other people that I do not know. I cannot understand why I am being sent to an O.T.U. and have a feeling that something is wrong. We have arrived by train at night and reported to Station H.Q. to be told to go to the airman's mess for a meal. We are then given hut numbers, allocated beds and told to report to the duty sergeant in the morning.

After a most uncomfortable night, I went to the airman's mess again for breakfast and on the way three Hurricane fighters took off low over my head. This confirmed my worst fears that whatever the reason was for me being posted to Sutton Bridge it was certainly not for flying. I have now reported to the sergeant at Station Head quarters and am told that we have been sent as ground defence and are to man Lewis guns which are in sand bagged enclosures spaced round the aerodrome.

The reason for this seems to be that the war is going very badly. The Germans have invaded most of Belgium and the large French Army appears to have collapsed. There is a strong risk that both these countries may capitulate. If this happens the aerodromes will be in danger of air attacks particularly in Norfolk. As each day passes I try to get an appointment to see the Commanding Officer or the Adjutant in an endeavour to find out how long I will be kept here but I cannot get past the sergeant who is really not interested. In desperation I have decided to write to the Station Commander at Cambridge. In the letter I have told him that I think there has been a mistake in my posting and that, after the farewell speech he gave us before we left, I find it difficult to believe that we were destined to go on ground defence.

A further ten days has elapsed without a reply to my letter but I was called into Staff headquarters this morning and told that I have been posted to Number 7 Elementary Flying Training School at Defford near Leicester with effect from 1st of May and can take a 48 hour pass. I will never know if my letter had any bearing on this posting.

Back in Horsforth I am able to tell Marie that living out is a strong possibility and she said she would look round and try to find someone for a short term let. I left again by train for Defford and found that it was a small grass aerodrome belonging to Boulton and Paul Ltd, the makers of the two seater fighters. They had accepted a contract from the RAF to supply all the facilities for Initial flying training. The aeroplanes are D.H. 82 Tiger Moths which are a later version of the Gipsy Moths which I had flown privately before the war. I was very pleased to find that Henry and Joe had already arrived here. The accommodation is comfortable and the food much better than the fare we have been used to, often a running buffet with a good selection of cold salads. The discipline too is much more relaxed and we are not expected to attend roll calls, only to be sure to attend flights at the right time each morning.

When I enquired about living out the Adjutant said he did not think this would be possible which was a big disappointment. However, in the evening I discovered that the man on guard duty at the gate was an old timer who did not seem to be concerned when we went out or came in and consequently decided to take a chance and make plans for Marie to come down. She had found a writer, a lady, who was looking for temporary accommodation and now arranged for her to lease the house so that she could join me. She found some pleasant people near the aerodrome who let us have rooms and I am able to join her after supper and return for breakfast without any questions asked.

The weather is much better now which is the reason for the German advance. The French Maginot line had been built many years ago and was supposed to be impregnable but the German armoured units circled round through Belgium. This left the British Expeditionary Force to rush forward in an attempt to hold the advance. It has also been announced that Winston Churchill is replacing Mr Chamberlain as Prime Minister.

I have enough experience to fly a Tiger Moth straight away but am told that I will have to carry out the full course as second pilot under Sergeant Ramsey for eight hours before I can go solo. The course consists of twenty two exercises.

It is now 24th July and I have been on the E.F.T.S. course for nearly six weeks, flying a total of 52 hours in Tiger Moths. The weather has been excellent and it has been a most enjoyable time. When not airborne, I have been able to spend a lot of time with Marie. Not only are the exercises we are required to do quite easy due to the lessons I had before the war but the relaxed discipline has made it almost like spending time in a flying club. This was not the case with many of the other trainees, some of whom suffered from air sickness, but I was quite surprised to see that even the worst afflicted got over it after a few flights. One notable example was a racing driver famous for his success at Brooklands who found these little aircraft very difficult. Flying did not come naturally to him but he struggled through the course and passed out successfully at the end. His name was Robin Hanson.

The large cloud over this happy time was the disastrous news from Europe. The fast moving German Panzer Divisions have occupied Paris and France is on the brink of surrender. Belgium has already capitulated and the British Expeditionary Force has been forced into a small area round Dunkirk which they have managed to hold. From here the Navy, Merchant navy and hundreds of small boats from harbours on the south coast have succeeded in rescuing a quarter of a million men and bringing them back to England.

We have been informed today that we are posted to Number 10 Advanced Training School at Ternhill to do the Initial Training School course which we have to complete prior to getting our wings and that we are to take 48 hours leave before reporting. Henry Heaton has a girlfriend, Joyce, who he has been courting for some time and has arranged to marry her in Leeds during this leave. Marie and I were invited so we stayed with my parents and had a very enjoyable day. It was whilst staying at Alwoodly Lane that a neighbour, Frank Moorhouse, told me that he wanted to sell his New Imperial motor cycle as he had little use for it. The bike was in excellent condition so I bought it off him and drove to Ternhill with Marie on the pillion. Ternhill is about five miles from Wellington where she was staying at a hotel but after I had been granted permission to live out she was able to rent some rooms for us near the aerodrome and later found rooms for Joyce to come down and stay with Henry.

The training aircraft are Avro Ansons which are obsolete for operations but ideal for training. They are twin engined machines and the first aircraft to have retractable undercarriages. The wheels are manually operated and have

27

to be wound up or down by the second pilot using a large handle. The course is expected to last about six weeks consisting of about 30 exercises, twelve of which are necessary before flying solo.

There is a lot of enemy activity at night which interferes with the night flying exercises so we practice instrument flying in the daytime by having a large pram type hood pulled over our heads and flying by sperry panel. This is a large panel mounted in the centre of the instrument panel with mostly giro operated instruments. On one of these exercises the instructor was pulling over the hood when the bar at the front knocked the two engine ignition switches and cut both engines. He did not notice what had happened so he had to search the ground for a suitable field as we were gliding down. I moved the hood and started winding down the wheels. We were now at about 4,000 feet and he side slipped and levelled out just clearing the hedge of a field to make a good landing, stopping just short of a ditch at the opposite side.

When we were safely down, he noticed the switches and said he would be in serious trouble for not noticing them earlier and that we must take off again. Otherwise an aircraft recovery team would have to be sent to remove the wings and load it onto a transporter. We got out and hauled the plane round. I swung the propellers so that he could taxi across the field to take off into the wind. Then we had to manhandle it again until the tail was near the hedge. Finally we climbed in and he opened up full throttle on both engines and released the brakes. We bounced our way across the field just skimming the hedge at the windward side before taking to the air. Once safely back at Ternhill, he asked me to keep the matter secret which I did.

Robin Hanson was also living out and his wife was having a baby. We would frequently meet them in a local pub for drinks in the evenings and he had a great sense of humour. He would tease Marie, calling her Mrs Moleskin because of a beige Corduroy trouser dress which she was wearing. He also used to keep telling her that she should have a Bambino. With war conditions as they are, it does not seem a sensible time to start a family but after a while Marie became keen on the idea so we decided we would.

It is now 8th September and I have completed the Initial training school course, having flown 37 hours bringing my total to 103 hours. I had a good pass, rated above average, and we are now entitled to wear wings on our uniforms. These are presented to us at a small ceremony after which we are to be notified of our promotions either to pilot officers or sergeant pilots. It is a great disappointment to me to find that I am not down for a commission and am only to be a sergeant pilot.

My father had always believed that it was most important to learn a trade and therefore I was educated at Roundhay High School which I left at fifteen. I had spent many years learning printing but, useful as it may have been for my future, it did not help when commissions were handed out. All the trainees without exception who had been to public schools became pilot officers. I felt very upset about this and asked to see the Adjutant, telling him that as I had done well on the course I expected a commission. He told me that these decisions were taken much higher up and that I would have to prove myself on a Squadron if I wanted one. I resolved that when I had children, I would make sure that they went to public schools.

At the beginning of September, I started the Advanced Training course (ATC), still at Ternhill. This is a fairly intense course mainly air to air camera gun exercises, Formation flying, Instrument flying, Night flying etc. The Night flying is badly interrupted by enemy intruders and most nights the exercises are cut short and the aerodrome blacked out for long periods. We often have to wait until three or four in the morning before flying can commence again. During this period, we had the opportunity to request to go onto either Fighters or Bombers. Henry Heaton and Ken Herridge chose to go onto Bombers and I decided on Fighters. I think Robin Hanson asked if he could go to Coastal Command but I never heard from him again after leaving Ternhill.

The course finished on 20th October. I now have a total of 152 hours flying and have been given 48 hours leave before reporting to Number 56 O.T.U. at Aston Down near Cheltenham. This is an operational training unit for Hurricane Fighters. We drove up to Chester for two days but as Marie is now showing distinct signs of her pregnancy, her mother thought she should not be riding on the back of a motor cycle. I therefore drove down to Aston Down and as soon as I was given permission to live out, I enquired at the local town, Stroud, for accommodation. I soon found rooms with a nice family and Marie came down by train. After selling the motor cycle to another pilot on the course, we saw an Austin seven Tourer advertised for sale in Cheltenham. After some negotiations, we bought this for £15.00.

I had about one hours dual on Harvards and then a few hours solo on Masters before going solo on a Hurricane. The weather has been very wet in this part of the country and as Aston Down is a grass aerodrome it has become very soft and boggy. After two incidents of wheels bogging in and tipping over on landing, it was decided to make the aerodrome unserviceable.

The course is now moved to Number 56 O.T.U. at Sutton Bridge near Kings Lynn in Norfolk where I had earlier spent a few weeks on ground defence. Marie and I drove here in the Austin and after being granted permission to live out, we decided to book in at the Sutton Bridge Hotel on the edge of the aerodrome. It is now 1st December and the course should take about four weeks to cover twenty exercises, including a good deal of formation flying, aerobatics, dog fighting and low flying. An old school friend of mine, Richard Branson, was on the course and also a friend of my sister, Harry Almond. Harry was also staying at the Bridge and one day he appeared covered in mud with his parachute over his shoulder, having bailed out and walked back over muddy fields. Apparently his engine had stopped. I never heard the reason for this but it was probably shortage of petrol and although we all viewed this with some amusement, I think it put him off Hurricanes.

The Spitfires and Hurricanes have inflicted severe losses on the German Bombers during September and October to such an extent that Hitler has postponed his plans for invading England for the time being. Field Marshall Goering who commands the Luftwaffe has assured Hitler that his large Bomber force could do such severe damage to the English towns and cities that we would be forced to surrender. As a result bombing has commenced and hundreds of aircraft are attacking London and the midlands on most nights without great loss.

We spent Christmas at the Bridge Hotel. On 29th December a Wing Commander came up from Group H.Q. to talk to us about the serious position that confronted the country. He explained to us that the only defences we had against night bombing were anti-aircraft guns in conjunction with searchlights, balloons or night-fighters. The guns were having a few successes but not enough. The problem was that even if they could be aimed right, the shells had to be timed to explode near the enemy and even if this was a few hundred feet above or below, it would not bring the plane down. Also bombers could sustain a good deal of shrapnel damage, even the loss of an engine and still get home. The raids on towns did not call for precision bombing and they were coming in at between 15,000 and 20,000 feet which was above the balloons.

The fighters are mainly Boulton and Paul Defiants, totally dependent on getting visuals silhouetted in the flames. By the time they got into firing range, the bomber would be in the dark taking evasive action and impossible to follow.

The Wing Commander told us that the most promising defence was Radar controlled fighters. The large Radar stations dotted down the East Coast could pick up incoming raids to within five or ten miles and when they were near the English Coast they would hand over to Ground Control Interception stations (G.C.I.). These were mobile and could be moved about the sector. They could pick up the Bombers and direct the fighters to within one or two miles. The Fighters carried an Air Interception operator and a small Radar set which could pick up a contact and direct the pilot to a range which should see the enemy even on the darkest nights. The purpose of his visit was to ask for volunteers to go to a Night Fighter Operational Training Unit to take the course in order to form more night fighter squadrons. I was intrigued with this new and most important development so I put my name forward along with three other pilots.

We finished the Hurricane course on 6th January and were granted 14 days leave before reporting to Number 54 Operational Training Unit at Church Fenton near Leeds. After spending a week with Marie's parents at Chester, we went to stay with my family at Alwoodley. This gave us the opportunity to look for accommodation near Church Fenton. We found a couple called the Claytons who had a Drapers shop in Tadcaster and who let us have rooms at their house.

The course started on 17th January and the aircraft were Blenheim 1s fitted with two Bristol Mercury V111 engines. These were day bombers first brought into service in the early thirties but now obsolete. They have been modified for night fighting by removing the hydraulic gun turret and fitting a seat and small radar set in the back. The aircraft is painted black, the armament is four Browning machine guns mounted under the nose and they have a top speed of between 200 and 220 miles per hour. Our Commanding Officer is Wing Commander Atcherley, one of two brothers famous in the RAF. He is a very determined man and although the weather is bad he is insistent that the night flying programme is not delayed. One day we had two or three feet of snow on the runways. It seemed inevitable that the night flying programme would be cancelled but he gave an order that everybody on the station should get out with shovels. This was not only aircrew and ground crew but all Station H.Q. Even the padre was asked to go out and help, such was the urgency to train night fighter pilots. After this great effort the runways were cleared and night flying continued.

I had put in an application for permissions to live out but was upset to find that this was turned down and I had to sleep in the sergeants' mess. Fortunately the Adjutant's wife was living in rooms next door to Marie and as they became friendly, Marie told her how disappointed she was particularly as her pregnancy was now well advanced. I think she must have asked her husband to speak to the C.O. because within two days I was granted permission to live out. On most mornings I now call on the Adjutant and give him a lift to the aerodrome.

It is now 3rd March and I have flown about 20 hours on Blenheims, 10 of which have been at night. The weather is still very bad and as the enemy seem to be aware that this is a night fighter training school they are paying us particular attention. The aerodrome has been bombed and strafed with machine gun fire on several occasions. Also one Blenheim has been shot down in the circuit and another damaged and forced to crash land.

Air gunners have now arrived at flights. They have been sent here to retrain as Air Interception operators. The word Radar is still highly secret and has not to be mentioned. My operator is Aircraftsman 2 Robbins, whose Christian name is Mitton which he does not like. Air gunners are often referred to as Tailend Charlies so he seems happy for me to call him Charlie in future. From now on we will be flying together, doing firstly daytime practice interceptions in pairs and then night time practice interceptions.

I soon found that Charlie was a very competent operator. He was seated in the back of the Blenheim where a small glass dome replaced the gun turret and he was able to look through a closed hood at the Air Interception set. This consists of two Cathode Ray tubes. One is horizontal and called the Elevation tube which shows a horizontal line with a ground echo at the right hand side. This limits the range to the height of the aircraft so that at 20,000 feet it could be as much as four miles. When the target was picked up, it showed as an echo on the line and would be longer at either the top or the bottom. The operator would instruct the pilot to climb or lose height until the echo was centralised. The right hand tube known as the Azimuth showed a vertical trace with the ground returns at the top and the echo would be either more on the left or the right. The operator would then call on the pilot to turn to port or starboard. He would also instruct the pilot to increase or decrease speed to bring the echo slowly down the line until the pilot got a visual. In the first instance this is usually exhaust pipes but it is essential to close in to identify the target as either friend or foe.

The system is very good but requires a lot of practice to avoid over corrections resulting in weaving and loss of overtaking speed. Also the serviceability leaves a lot to be desired, with interceptions being broken off because sets were 'on the blink'.

I have now completed the course which comprised 22 exercises and my total flying hours are 240. The date is the end of March and I am posted to Number 68 squadron which is being reformed as a Night Fighter squadron at Catterick and am given another 48 hour pass before reporting. Marie is now getting very advanced with her pregnancy so I decide that it is better for me to drive her back to Chester until the baby arrives. I call at Church Fenton on the return and pick up Charlie and Walley Barker, a friend of mine who is also posted to Catterick with his operator Tom. It is a small pre-war grass aerodrome on the side of the north road and we are allocated a house in the airmens' married quarters which we share. The Commanding Officer is Wing Commander Max Aitken who is the son of Lord Beaverbrook, the Minister of Aircraft Production. The squadron is not yet operational and our time is spent on practice interception exercises until the aircraft are brought up to strength. It it now 14th April and the C.O. has told us that we are moving to High Ercall near Wellington where we will be put on defensive operations. High Ercall is a new aerodrome. Bulldozers have cleared good runways but the earth has been pushed into large mounds at the edge. We are billeted in wooden huts and again I share one with Walley Barker, Charlie and Bob Varley.

Most of our aircraft are still Blenheims but we are slowly being re-equiped with Beaufighters which are specially designed for night fighting. The cockpit is very near the nose with excellent vision through a bulletproof windscreen. They are powered by two Bristol Hercules engines and double row air cooled, developing over 1000 Hp each. The armament is four 20 millimeter Canons mounted under the fuselage carrying explosive and incendiary shells and six .303 Browning Machine guns in the wings. They have a speed in excess of 300 miles per hour. The only fault is that they have a nasty swing to port on landing when the engines are throttled back. This has to be corrected by applying the starboard brake as soon as the wheels touch the ground. These machines are in very short supply and although I am sure Max Aitken is using all the influence he can with his father, most of the patrols have to be carried out in Blenheims.

The enemy are now carrying out heavy night raids on Liverpool and the I.C.I. factories on Merseyside, flying up through our sector at 10,00 to 15,000 feet, then diving down to release their bombs before making a getaway over the sea and round Wales. On one or two occasions we were put on to these by our Group Control Interception station and Charlie was able to get contacts on his Air Interception set but our speed was insufficient to close in on them before they had reached Liverpool. The engines had an override button which gave them extra power though only to be used for five minutes. At one time I had this pressed for a quarter of an hour in an attempt to close the range. The result was that the exhaust rings which surrounded the engines were red hot and would have shown up like neon rings if we had managed to get close to the enemy.

When I landed from an air test on 20th May, there was a message for me to say that Marie had gone into Chester Hospital to have her baby. I applied for a 48 hour pass but by the time I arrived at the hospital Marie had given birth. She had a fairly painful time and I was sorry not to be with her earlier. Unfortunately although her mother had been able to run her in she could not stay owing to pressure of work at the hotel. When I got there she was looking quite well and holding a beautiful baby girl. She had decided that she would like her to be called Yvette. We agreed that she would be better remaining at home for two weeks before finding rooms in Wellington.

The bombing of Liverpool is still continuing but as we still have very few Beaufighters we are not getting any successes. The Germans have started using a Pathfinder method. The idea of this is that their most experienced pilots go in first and drop fire bombs on the target whilst the inexperienced pilots follow on and drop their bombs on the fires.

I have managed to get a night off on 28th May and have driven up to Marie's home, the Stamford Bridge hotel, to see her. We were sitting with her parents in the Lounge when the sirens went off and we heard aircraft overhead. I tried to assure them that the Germans would not be bombing Chester and that the target would be Liverpool Docks or the

I.C.I. factories on Merseyside. This proved to be wrong when fields at the back of the house were heavily bombed. It seems that the pathfinder had mistaken the river Dee for the Mersey as it was a misty night and the other bombers had released their bombs on the fires. Fortunately there was not much damage done as they fell on open country. I think this gave our defence people an idea because shortly after they deliberately lit fires on the Welsh hills and the inexperienced pilots dropped all theirs on these fires which saved Liverpool for that night.

1st June turned out to be a bad day for me. I was waiting at "B" Flight for the flying detail when the Flight Commander, Flight Lieutenant Major came in and said that the C.O. had found a Beaufighter at Gatwick which he wanted collected and that he was to fly me there to bring it back. It was not a new machine and had been used by Coastal Command but was to be fitted with Air Interception equipment for night fighting purposes. When we arrived at Gatwick, Flight Lieutenant Major pointed to the Beaufighter at the other side of the field and told me to collect it. He then turned round and took off again.

The Beaufighter looked as if it had been left for some time in the rain but I found the Ground Crew, signed the form and got them to start the engines. All aircraft engines have a dual ignition system with dual spark plugs to each cylinder and an important test is to run each engine separately to maximum revolutions whilst the chocks are under the wheels and switch off each system in turn. The engines should drop 150 to 200 revolutions and should not be flown if the mag drop, as it is called, is above this. Both engines had drops of over 400 revs and I should have got out and had it serviced but I knew how desperate Max Aitken was to get these Beaufighters so I decided to take a chance and fly it carefully back. I flew slowly and the flight back to High Ercall was quite smooth but when I landed it gave the usual swing to port and I applied the starboard brake only to find that it was not working. The aircraft swung off the runway and headed for one of the earth mounds which had been cleared from the runway. The machine ran up the side of one of these, damaging the undercarriage and coming to rest on the top. From my position on top of this hill I could see Max Aitken's office below the watch tower and saw him run to his car and drive over to me. He was obviously very annoyed and not interested in my explanation. I told him that I was familiar with the swing problem and would like to have the starboard brake tested but this was to no avail. The worst thing about the incident was that it put me in the bad books of the C.O. and for the next three weeks all my patrols were on Blenheims.

Marie is now fit enough to live out with me again so I drove to Chester to collect her and Yvette and we found rooms with a young couple in Wellington. Unfortunately, after Yvette got onto a bottle she started waking up and crying at about three or four o'clock in the morning and although the owners of the house were understanding about it, the husband had long working hours and ran a risk of losing his job if we stayed, so we had to offer to move. The trouble was that the midwife at the Nursing home believed in sticking rigidly to the rules. She had told Marie that on no account must she exceed the prescribed dose even though Yvette was obviously hungry. We saw a doctor however, who said it was alright to give her more and after that she slept right through the nights.

In the meantime we had found rooms with a German couple who had left Germany when Hitler began to persecute the Jews. It seems that they had a big general store in Berlin and sold everything up to come to England because they were Jewish.

Max Aitken's operator, Jack Higham, was living out with his wife Betty next door and Marie became friendly with her. My night duties are now two nights on and two off but I have to report every day to do air tests. The squadron has now been totally re-equipped with Beaufighter 1's and they all have to have extensive testing. The Air interception equipment has to be set up by doing practice interceptions in pairs. They are a great improvement on the Blenheims from a performance and armament point of view but they are not stable to operate which makes instrument flying more tedious. At the present time the weather is very good and the nights clear but this may be a problem in winter conditions.

We have been keeping up night operations through June and there have been two enemy aircraft destroyed by the Squadron but the raids on Liverpool across our section have been tapering off and more bombers have been coming up the Welsh coast and coming into Liverpool over the sea. It is therefore decided to send a detachment to RAF Valley which is on the Isle of Anglesey and I am to be sent there from 7th July for a week.

It has been an uneventful week. On 9th July we had a long patrol until dawn with two abortive contacts on low flying aircraft but at this height the range of our Air Interceptors was too small to be effective. I returned to High Ercall on 15th July and resumed our nightly patrols with our Ground Control Interception station and also Searchlight Cooperation. There is less enemy activity largely because Hitler seems to have abandoned his plan for invading England and has declared war on Russia who was previously his ally. This has resulted in some Luftwaffe Squadrons being moved from France to his new eastern front.

In the squadron "A" Flight, we have four Polish pilots and operators who managed to escape to England when their country was occupied and although they are good pilots there are language difficulties, particularly with control. One of these crews has just been killed when he flew into a large hill called Wrekin which is close to the circuit. This occurred on a misty night and probably because of this it was decided to install a blind approach system at High Ercall. This means that we will have to go on a Blind Approach course at Watchfield. It is a ten day course and I have to go on 8th September.

When I returned I was told that it had been decided to form a Polish Flight and that I was to be moved to 255 Squadron based at Coltishall in Norfolk, along with Walley Barker and our operators. 255 Squadron will be sending their Polish pilots in exchange. I have been given a week's leave before reporting there and am able to run Marie and Yvette to Chester until arrangements can be made for them to join me again.

255 Squadron are equipped with Beaufighter 1's which are fitted with Merlin water cooled engines instead of the Bristol air cooled Radial engines for which they are designed. The Merlins protude further out in front of the wings which does not help the stability problem and because the propellers rotate in the opposite direction, the swing on landing is to starboard. The reason for the change is because the Bristol aero-engine factory has been bombed and Merlins have to be used until the correct ones are in production again.

Coltishall is a good station about ten miles from Norwich and near the Norfolk Broads. It was built before the war and still has a grass airfield. Charlie was promoted to sergeant in July so we live in the sergeants' mess until I can make other arrangements. Shortly after arrival I asked to see the C.O., Wing Commander Winsor to gain permission to live out and went to his office which is situated on the edge of the aerodrome. In front of his window was a Beaufighter tipped over with a collapsed undercarriage. He said, "You will have to watch the swing on landing, Greaves, it is very vicious as I found out last night."

I bring up my request to live out but he gives me a firm refusal adding, "This is a man's war and we cannot be distracted by wives. I have sent mine to Canada for the duration." This is a great disappointment but I am considering getting Marie to come down so that we can be together on my time off. Walley Barker has already brought his wife and new baby here but is not allowed to live out with her.

I am in "B" Flight and the Flight Commander is Squadron Leader Player. He is an Australian, an excellent man, well respected by all and generally known as Johnnie. When I reported to him, he said I should immediately get in some experience on the new Beaufighter 11's so I took off and did several circuits and landings and had a good look at the area. After half an hour a low ground fog closed in. Apparently these are not unusual in Norfolk at this time of year. The fog totally obscured the ground apart from the very top of the Watch office, so I flew over this and set course down-wind for about two miles. I then turned onto a reciprocal course and reduced height almost to ground level and as soon as I identified the boundary, I throttled back and did an excellent landing. I taxied back to Flights to find a very relieved Johnnie Player and the maintenance chief Warrant officer, Elcoates, waiting for me. They had obviously been fearing the worst. Johnnie Player congratulated me on a good landing under such difficult conditions. I think it may have been to do with this incident that he recommended me to the C.O. for a commission. When it came through two weeks later, I was allowed to move across into the Officers' Mess. Life is very different here. In the sergeants' mess, it was rather dominated by regular Flight Sergeants and Warrant Officers or ground staff from Station H.Q. and maintenance who reserved their rights to special chairs in the mess and access to the Billiard tables. Sergeant Pilots and Radio Operators were in a small minority there and it was not the thing to discuss flying matters.

In the Officers' quarters, I am provided with my own room, a comfortable bed and the use of a batman to clean my shoes and polish buttons etc. In the Mess, I am on friendly terms with the C.O. and Flight Commanders and the food is a great improvement. Previously I had to attend pay parades each week but now it is paid into my account monthly and all drinks at the bar are put on my Mess bill. Any rail travel is also first class. I am making many new friends here. Hugh Wyrill, Sandy Ballantine, Cameron Cox, Mike Gloster and many others. When I tell Marie the news, I suggest that she comes down with Yvette and finds somewhere local to live so that I can see her in my time off. She is keen to do this and stays at a local hotel while looking for rooms. Coltishall is only a small village so she is able to push Yvette round in the pram. It is while doing this that she notices a large house in its own grounds on the outskirts and in desperation decides to call and enquire. The owner is called Mrs Witteringham and she tells Marie that she is not accustomed to letting rooms, to which Marie replies that she is not accustomed to looking for them but the war makes it necessary. She is the wife of the late Bishop of Ipswich who died a few years ago. The discussion and particularly the sight of Yvette in a pram makes her think and she decides to let us have two rooms. Sometime later an army officer's wife called and she agreed to let her have a room as well. Fortunately, she was interested in the garden, which was large and neglected and she produced all manner of dishes at a time when vegetables were very scarce.

The enemy activity over England is much reduced and the big massed bomber raids have given way to intruder patrols over airfields and factories. It is October, the weather is very bad and we are required to keep up standing patrols over the North Sea. The intruders seem to take advantage of this weather to protect themselves against fighters. Long patrols in these circumstances put a great strain on the pilots as they are required to concentrate continuously on the Flying instruments in completely blacked out conditions which tends to defy all natural instincts. To an experienced pilot, general flying, turning, banking, diving and climbing are as natural as they are for a bird but in this situation the readings of six flying instruments must be rigidly followed. At 300 miles per hour a slight ease forward of the control column can tighten the straps on your shoulders giving a sensation of being upside down; also lack of bank in a turn can throw you to one side. I think that the bad run of accidents we are having in the winter months is probably due to people giving way to natural instincts. In Bomber command the Aircraft are fitted with automatic pilots which can fly the aircraft on set courses but these are never fitted to Fighters.

I came down to breakfast one morning after a night off to receive the news that the C.O., Wing Commander Winsor, has crashed into the sea in the night whilst on patrol.

In early November Wally Barker and I are ordered to patrol on a particularly bad night. I was to fly out to sea south of Chromer and Walley to the north. The thick cloud was made worse by the presence of Cumulo Nimbus clouds known to us as Cunims. In daylight, these are like giant mushrooms with a strong up current in the centre which converts rain to hail at the top and then falls from the outside. When you fly through them, apart from the violent bumping, the static electricity plays on the windscreen giving an extra distraction.

I had flown through two of these when Operations call me up to say that they are not getting any reply from Walley and will I go to the position where they had last heard of him. I did this by reducing height down to one thousand feet and I saw then that the cloud was lit up by flames which are coming from the sea. I reported this to Operations and resumed my patrol. I am sure that Walley must have lost his concentration in one of these treacherous clouds and spun into the water.

Wing Commander Kelley is now our Commanding Officer and the next day he sees me in the Mess and says he understands that I was a friend of Walley's and would be glad if I could call on his wife who he gathers lives nearby. She has been informed by wire but he is sure she would appreciate a visit. During the conversation I take the liberty of asking if I can have permission to live out and thankfully he says there will be no problem. In the evening I take Marie with me to see her and we are surprised to find that she is bearing up very well.   This is because the wire had only said that Walley was missing. As he had gone into the sea, no body could be recovered and the Air Ministry could not pronounce him as dead. We comfort her as much as we can and try to tell her not to build her hopes up too high but we leave her quite convinced that he will come back.

Our bombing raids over Germany are getting larger and there are many returning stragglers who have lost radio contact returning through our sector. On two occasions in November and December we are scrambled to chase bogies which turn out to be Wellingtons.

Marie is settling down at the big house and is making a few friends in the village. Now with two nights on and two off, we are able to spend more time together but unfortunately I am flying over Christmas and will only be able to have a few hours with her on Boxing day. The friends we have met near Coltishall have an enclosed Austin 7 which they want to sell because they cannot get enough petrol and, as we find our car rather cold for Yvette, we decide to buy it. Charlie says he would like an open Austin so we in turn sell ours to him. We do get a moderate petrol allowance but as I park my car near our Beaufighter at night, the ground crew will usually top it up when they have filled the Beau. The aviation fuel is one hundred octane, not ideal for an Austin 7 but it seems to work.

On New Years Eve I had ten days leave so we drove across to Chester and then to Leeds for a few days. Before we left, Marie found that she was having another baby. Her mother and sister, Nan, are rather concerned and think that she has enough to cope with, travelling around with Yvette but Marie is very happy at the prospect and seems to have no doubt that I will survive the war.

January is a bad month for the squadron. We had a new Flight Commander in "A" Flight but within a week he crashed and was killed whilst on patrol. Later in the month, I was waiting for the previous patrol to land one night when I noticed that it was on the wrong line of approach. It was a very misty night and he must have misread the approach lights. It was Flight Lieutenant Jimmy Dale who was a regular pilot before the war and had been in the Battle of Britain. I heard a swishing noise as he flew into a wood at the side of the aerodrome but unusually there was no fire. I told Operations that I was going to investigate and taxi back to flights. I stopped the engines and drove in my car with Charlie to the edge of the wood. It was very dark but we have two strong torches and followed a trail of broken branches on foot.

We came upon a track where whole trees had been uprooted and finally found the Beau with its nose smashed in reared up against a very large trunk. I shone my torch up to the pilot's seat and saw Jimmy's crushed and beheaded body. I then heard some groaning from the back and tell Charlie to hurry back and bring the ambulance. The top hatch was broken but I managed to climb in to find the Operator still on his seat. He was bent over so that his head was almost touching the ground. I struggled to release him and laid him on the floor. He was still conscious but his face was badly damaged. I tried to comfort him as much as I could until the medics arrived with stretchers. I helped to ease him out through the small hatch so that they could take over. The Station Commander also arrived and put a ladder up to the nose in order to lift what remained of Jimmy Dale onto a stretcher. Charlie and I drove back to Flights to be told that we had to take off and resume our patrol.

On the 27th January, I have to leave Marie for three weeks as a detachment is being sent to West Malling in Kent to help out with the defence of London. My patrols there are uneventful but Cameron Cox manages to shoot down a

Dornier 217 which is the first success the squadron has had with the Beaufighters.

We return to Coltishall on 16th February and are now informed that the squadron is to change bases with 68 Squadron and move to High Ercall from the beginning of March which means that Marie will have to move back again. After flying my plane to High Ercall, I get a lift back so that I can drive her and Yvette to Wellington. We are lucky to find a family that have just moved from South Africa into a large house. They agree to rent rooms to us and Marie settles down there very well.

There is little activity now in this sector and we spend most nights doing practice interceptions with a new Ground Control Interception station called Hack Green. Fortunately new Beaufighter VI's are now coming out with Bristol engines and the squadron is gradually re-equipping with these. Also they have tail-planes slightly angled upwards in place of the horizontal ones. These are called di-hedral tail-planes and they have made the Beaufighters much more stable. On one or two nights, because of raids on Coventry, we have to support a sector to the south which is called Ground Control Interception Cumberton and during this time Hugh Wyrill and Sergeant Willins shoot down a Junkers 88.

In December two major events have happened. First the Japanese have bombed Pearl Harbour doing considerable damage to two major American battleships. Secondly, they have made landings in Malaya and bombed Singapore. The outcome of these actions is that America has declared war not only on Japan but also on Germany and Italy. We are also at war with Japan. All this is rather disturbing but at least we have the might of America with us which ensures that we shall win in the end.

April and May are very uneventful months. All the nights are spent on interception exercises with various GCI stations and as the weather is now good we do not have any more accidents. On 26th May I have to go on a three day course to Wittering which is an update on blind approach and night vision. On my return, I am told that the squadron will be moving to RAF Honiley which is better placed for the defence of Birmingham and Coventry. We decide that it would be better for Marie to return to the Stamford Bridge Hotel for the time being as she is now heavily pregnant, so I drive her and Yvette up to Chester before moving.

At Honiley we have some active patrols but the enemy raids are mostly single aircraft and the only interceptions we have turn out to be friendly. Hugh Wyril does claim two damaged on a night when there is more activity than usual. The new Beaufighter and the latest Air Interception equipment is a great improvement and it is regrettable that we did not have this equipment when the cities were suffering so badly a year or more ago.

We are being warned that the Squadron will be sent overseas in the coming months and if this is the case it would be better for Marie to move back into our house at Horsforth after our new baby arrives. I have been told by her mother that it should be due at the end of August but I think she is giving me a later date to avoid me worrying.

On the morning of 10th August I am woken up early by a WAAF to tell me that I have a daughter. I say that this was far too soon but she assures me it is true. I go to see Johnnie Player who says I can take a few days off so I drive straight to the hospital in Chester to find Marie sitting up in bed with a lovely little baby. She comes back to the Bridge after a day or two and we agree that, as it was now certain that we are going overseas, the best thing would be for her to move back to our house in Horsforth. Her mother employs a girl called Edna at the Bridge and as she is worried about Marie living on her own with the babies, she persuades her to come to Horsforth as a help.

On 19th September (1942) the Squadron ceases to be operational and all our time is spent on training exercises and petrol endurance tests to be sure that the planes can fly to Africa when necessary. The Air Interception equipment is still very secret and must not be flown over enemy territory so it looks as if this will have to go out by sea.

On 28th September I get fourteen days embarkation leave so we drive to Leeds and call at our house. We are both appalled at the terrible state it is in. The writer who had rented it has a very unkempt dog which has left hairs on carpets, furniture and beds and the place is so dirty and untidy that we give her three days to vacate it and she does not argue. We stay with my parents for three days before moving in and giving it a thorough clean. I leave the car in the garage and return to Honiley by train.

NORTH AFRICA

255 Squadron

10 November: The squadron is now definitely moving overseas but at the moment everybody seems to be completely in the dark regarding our destination. There are of course hundreds of rumours going about but, as far as I can see, very little foundation for them.

We have been re-equipped with new Beaufighter VI's with di-hedrial tailplanes. These are quite an improvement on our old ones, being more stable to fly, slightly faster and fitted with long range tanks, giving them a total tankage of 600 gallons. We have also obtained tropical equipment and army type battle dress, so the general feeling is that we shall be going to the Middle East. General Montgomery, in command of the British forces in Egypt, has just launched a big offensive which is pushing the German and Italian troops back into Libya. Also some British and American forces have landed at various points in French Morocco to attack the Germans in the rear. It seems obvious that we are going to play some part in these operations. We have been non-operational for several weeks now and our time has been spent in doing long range flights in our Aircraft to test their petrol consumption. My new aircraft is letter "p" after its three predecessors and both Charlie and I are very satisfied with its performance. He is swatting up navigation and morse etc. which will be necessary for our flight out. We all go to untold trouble to get the best out of these machines and spend quite a few hours each day in sand papering and polishing them to reduce the air resistance and obtain the maximum speed.

A week ago I returned from 17 days embarkation leave but as it went so very quickly, I have been hoping it will be possible to see Marie again for a few hours. Today I thought of a suitable scheme and asked the C.O. if I could fly the Magister up to Yeadon to collect some luggage, this being the best excuse I can muster.

The weather is rather misty and I have considerable difficulty in navigating to Yeadon, particularly past Derby and Sheffield, but finally put down at Yeadon at twelve o'clock. It is unfortunate that my stay will have to be very short as the C.O. said he required the Maggie at 3 o'clock. My old civilian flying instructor, Captain Warrel, is a Chief Test Pilot at Yeadon so I go into his office to have a word with him and ring for a taxi at the same time.

I had flown over our house rather low, so I meet Marie walking up towards the aerodrome. She is wearing the new hat that I sent her and looks very nice. I have only half an hour that I can spend with her so I arrange for the taxi to call back again. It is marvellous to see her but the time goes much too quickly and, in what seems like a matter of minutes the wretched taxi driver is hooting his horn to tell me of his return. Little Yvette just sat and watched me all the time. I am sure she must think I am a funny sort of daddy. Marie comes up to the aerodrome to see me off and the guards allow her to come up to the Watch office. I have some trouble starting but finally get away at about two o'clock. It is very depressing to watch Marie's figure get smaller and smaller. I fly low over our house and take a last look at it before settling down to my map reading through the mist back to Honiley. It is a little late when I get back but the C.O. does not comment on it.

The following day, 11th November, several of us go on what is known as a "Battle Inoculation" course so we are up at 7.00 am to catch a 7.30 transport which takes us to some army training grounds several miles from the aerodrome. The idea of the course is to get people used to battle conditions. We are given rifles and told to advance across a field, line abreast, five paces apart. Some machine gunners fire bullets between us as we walk along and explosions take place near us at various points. It is quite exciting.

"B" Flight now consists of the following; firstly our Flight Commander, Squadron Leader Player (Johnnie). He is an extremely good type and one of the most solid, likable people I have ever met. He has the utmost consideration for all his crews at all times.

Flight Lieutenant Dunning White, or Peter, is unfortunately going out by boat for medical reasons. Peter fought in the Battle of Britain and has a DFC. He is a very good sport.

Next comes Hugh - Flying Officer Wyrill. He is one of the squadron's first pilots and has just been awarded a DFC for operations with the squadron. He is a very keen flyer.

Flying Officer Tony Kerch has recently had some bad luck. During a night flying test several months ago he had an engine cut and crash landed in a field. His operator was killed and Tony was burned. He was in hospital for some time but is quite fit again now. His operator is now Flight

Sergeant Wall or Hank, and they will be flying out. Pilot Officer Stephen or Steve is completely mad. He is always in trouble with the C.O. for low flying but, apart from this, he is a very good pilot. Many people say that he would have killed himself by now if he wasn't.

Pilot Officer Kendall was a flight Sergeant and has just got his commission. He is notable for his tall stories and is accepted as the biggest line-shooter in the squadron. This is probably because he has spent quite a number of years in Singapore and has always some story to tell about it. His operator is Pilot Officer Charlie Hill. He was a butcher before the war and is a very blunt, good natured sort of bloke. He was an air gunner on Defiants before joining the squadron.

Pilot Officer O'Sullivan is, as his name denotes, an Irishman. He is a very good character to have on a squadron. His operator is Pilot Officer Bob Griffiths. He is quite as popular as his pilot.

Flying Officer Gloster (Mike) has just joined the squadron and will be flying out with Pilot Officer Oswald as his operator. Pilot Officers Weston and Hills are also new comers who will be going out by boat, as will Sergeant Clark, a recent arrival from an Operational Training Unit.

Flight Sergeant Johnnie Willins is Hugh's operator. He is a Scotsman and a very genial type. He received a Distinguished Flying Medal when Hugh got his Distinguished Flying Cross.

Johnnie Player's operator is Flying Officer Wynzar, or Ronnie, and Peter's operator is Pilot Officer Kane, usually called Cobber after his namesake, the "Ace"

I have not yet mentioned Charlie, my operator, Warrant Officer Robbins. We have flown together for over two years now and I should feel distinctly uncomfortable flying at night if Charlie was not in the back. He is a tee-totaller and a man of very good principles.

Everybody is keyed up ready to go now and we are expecting to fly to Portreath, which will be our jumping off point, tomorrow. Ground crews are busy putting the finishing touches to our aircraft and we have spent the day checking our equipment.

Today is the 12th November and rain and low cloud prevent us taking off for Portreath as arranged. We spend the whole day waiting for it to clear but finally give it up as a bad job at 3.0 o'clock. However the next day, Friday 13th November, is fine and we finally take off. There are lots of last minute things to see to but we get away at 11.0 o'clock.

Portreath is near Land's End and we all get there alright with the exception of Tony Kerch who is held up with engine trouble. We have plenty of work to do when we land after we have found our billets and had a meal. We go along to the Briefing room to find out all about our trip. For the first time we are told we are going somewhere near Algiers, but have to land at Gibraltar to refuel. It is about 1,250 miles to Gibraltar taking a route round Spain. This gives us a small margin of spare petrol but would not cope with getting lost so our course must be accurate. We draw what seems to be hundreds of maps and all get down to work, planning our respective courses. Charlie and I work until 9.0 o'clock, after which time we are quite happy about the trip which we are to do the following morning. Hugh has also finished so we compare notes and go to the mess for some food.

Apart from us, there is a squadron of Bisleys going out tomorrow morning so at dinner the mess is very full and there are many opinions exchanged about the best way of getting to Gibraltar. Hugh and I finish our dinner, have a beer and go to the room which we are sharing. I only feel to have been asleep about five minutes when the Batman wakens me and says it is 3.0 o'clock. We get dressed quickly and go to the mess for breakfast. It is very dark but the weather is quite good.

After breakfast we go to the briefing room where I meet Charlie. He has already got the Met forecast which does not look too good down the Portuguese coast. He works out the course taking into account the new wind whilst I go out to my aircraft and run it up. I am feeling happier after this when I find everything in order. It is surprising how much confidence I now have in this aircraft.

I meet Hugh again - his aircraft is OK so we go back to the Briefing room. The C.O. is there. He is not very pleased with the Met forecast but, as he knows that we are urgently required at Algiers, he decides that we shall go. Charlie has worked out the new courses so we collect our rations and thermos flasks and go out to the aircraft. There are three people to take off before me so I wait until they have disappeared into the night before I taxi out onto the flare path. Once off the ground I turn on to the first course which is to the Scillies. It is a moonlit night and I can see the coast line as we go out to sea.

In a matter of fifteen minutes we can see the dark shapes of the Scillies below us, so we set our second course which takes us right across the Bay of Biscay to the north west coast of Spain. This is nearly a three hour leg, entirely over the sea. The weather is not good and we have to fly at 500 feet above the rough unfriendly waves in the Bay.

As we get nearer Spain, the weather improves and we make a landfall just a little after schedule. It is a very pleasant sight to see the sun on the coast and, for the next hour and a half, I continue map reading down the shoreline. At 11.30 am Charlie comes forward and we have our rations and tea from thermos flasks. The trip was planned to go round the coast of Spain and Portugal but we were told that if our petrol was getting low we could fly over Portugal at 10,000 feet.

We have been making petrol calculations and as we have used a little more than expected we decide to take a short cut. We do this just after passing Lisbon by cutting across to Faro. We hit the coast again here and fly across the bay past Cadiz to Trafalgar Bay, where Nelson's famous battle was fought. From here we follow the coast round through the Straits and at last see the Rock ahead of us. It is a very impressive sight, sticking straight up over a thousand feet above the sea. We approach the nose of the rock and fire off the correct coloured vary lights. We receive the OK signal and fly round the rock to the runway. In doing so we pass over the harbour where there seems to be hundreds of ships of all classes.

The runway is built across the narrow peninsula which joins the rock to Spain and is built out over the sea at one side and runs to the edge of the Mediterranean at the other, so special care has to be taken when landing. The aerodrome is terribly crowded with aircraft parked all over the place. The trip has taken just over six hours and we are pleased to get out to stretch our legs. Everybody else comes in without problems except one Bisley which had engine trouble and had to crash land in Portugal.

We learn that we are to take off at 10 o'clock tomorrow, 15th November for Maison Blanche so, after having a meal, Hugh and I go out to have a look round. It is a peculiar little town. Most of the shops are Spanish but many things can be bought that are unobtainable in England. I manage to send a cable to Marie, telling her I have arrived. We get great amusement out of buying a banana since they are very plentiful here. Cigarettes are also very cheap so I buy 800 to take with me.

At night, Group Captain Atcherley, who is going to be our Sector Commander invites us to the Rock Hotel to have dinner with him. After eating we have several drinks on the balcony overlooking the bay. It is a beautiful star-lit night and a memorable sight looking out over the harbour at the little Spanish towns without blackouts on the other side of the bay.

We are up early on the morning of the 15th and are briefed for the last leg. It is a very nice day and we take off at the time arranged. I fly most of the way at 500 feet. The Mediterranean looks very calm and very blue as we race over it at 250 miles per hour. After two hours we make a landfall on the North African coast near Oran. From here I fly along the coast for another hour before sighting Algiers. It looks a very clean city from the air with tall white buildings. I have little difficulty locating the aerodrome which seems to be crowded with Spitfires, American Lightnings and C.47 Paratroop transports. We go in and land, then taxi up to where several other of our Beaufighters are parked. The terrain is rough compared with English aerodromes and shows recent signs of fighting and bombing. On landing we find that the place had only been captured four days previously.

It is quite hot now so I change into shorts and an open shirt. The country here is bleak, the ground bare and the only things that seem to grow on it are thistles and cacti. We picket our aircraft and wait for the others to land before moving off to search for signs of life.

Johnnie Player lands and we walk across the aerodrome with him to a dirty hut which is sick quarters. Outside we find a bewildered looking doctor who tells us that the country is ridden with Typhus and Typhoid, that we must not drink the water and should beware of bugs. He has lots of moans about having no equipment. We ask him where we can eat and he says the only way is to try to collar a truck and go down to the docks at Algiers where we might get some Compo rations. Not happy with this we walk round and find that some Spitfire boys, who arrived a day or two ago, have organised a Frenchman in a little café to cook some RAF food. We manage to knuckle in on this and get some stew. After eating we are faced with the problem of getting our aircraft serviceable for the night. We have no ground crew so we have to see to our own machines.

Hugh and I manage to commandeer a lorry and drive round the aerodrome looking for petrol dumps. These turn out to be just collections of four gallon tins tipped at different locations round the site. No one is in charge so we load our lorry with about 600 gallons in tins and go in search of an ammunition dump. This is a similar sort of place so again we stock up with a few thousand rounds of machine gun bullets and cannon shells.

We drive up to our aircraft and it takes Charlie and I about six hours to re-arm and re-fuel our machine. One can imagine what a task it is filling an aircraft with 300 gallons of petrol from four gallon tins. After this we go and have some more stew for tea and try and find somewhere to sleep. The only place seems to be a dirty building with a concrete floor. We have no beds and only three blankets so the prospect of sleeping on the floor is not very appealing. When the Wing Commander tells us that we are not on readiness tonight, we go to the hut and try to sleep. What is more disturbing than the concrete floor is the number of bugs and lice in the building. I have a most unpleasant night as apart from the discomfort of the floor, it gets extremely cold after midnight. We get up and have stew for breakfast again. There were a few bombs dropped near the aerodrome during the night but no damage was done.

The morning of **16th November** is spent doing inspections on our aircraft. With not having any ground crews, it is almost a full time job for Charlie and I to keep our Beau serviceable. Apparently last night the Hun dropped a number of booby traps, such as pencils and food tins etc. which blow up when handled. During the day at least six airmen are seriously injured by these things.

We do our first night's readiness tonight so Charlie and I take off at 6.30 on patrol. There are a few Huns around but as we have not got our equipment yet we are unable to see anything. We fly for one and a half hours and then come in to land. Hugh also does a short patrol during the night.

17 November: I get up at about 10 o'clock and have a bath in a stone trough near the hut. We are not on readiness at night so Hugh and I go into Algiers before lunch. We have a meal there which chiefly consists of vegetables (there is no meat in Algiers). We have a bottle of wine which is very cheap here, about the equivalent of one shilling and six pence per bottle.

We walk round the town in the afternoon where we meet Tony and Johnnie Player. In the evening we go and have a drink at the Le Paris hotel. At 11 o'clock we walk down to the docks and get a lift back on a lorry. There is a continual stream of vehicles going past the aerodrome to the front so we have no difficulty finding one. I have a slightly better night because I have put about eight petrol tins together to make a bed. These feel softer than concrete but the other chaps complain about the noise I make when I turn over.

18 November is rather uneventful, we are still eating at the little café and our only complaint is that we do not get enough food. I break a tooth on a date stone and spend the afternoon searching Algiers for an American field dentist. I find one at Fort De L'Eau and he fixes the problem for me. We are on duty again at night and do another patrol. The Huns are over Algiers again but as before we are unable to see any of them. We landed after about one and a half hours and slept in the operations room.

19 November: Hugh, Tony, Johnnie Player and I go into Algiers again. We have a meal and some wine at Le Paris. This seems to be the best place to go although we never get anything more than vegetables. During the evening two drunken American officers pick a fight with one another and Tony and I have the job of throwing them out. Luckily they are too drunk to put up much resistance. It is raining when we emerge so we go to the French Police station and try to get a taxi. The Police are very helpful but we have to argue with a driver before he will take us because there is a raid on and he wants to be in a shelter.

20 November is probably one of the blackest days of the squadron's history. Hugh and I spend the morning getting our aircraft serviceable and in the afternoon give our machines an air test. The C.O. has managed to requisition a little hotel about a mile from the aerodrome for an Officer's mess. We are to move into it tomorrow so Hugh and I spend the afternoon packing our kit again.

We are in readiness at night and have an early tea. Hugh is the first off so he has to go to the operations room at 5.30 pm. I am walking along, following him, at 6.30 pm just about dusk when I hear some strange aircraft overhead. A second later there is a colossal explosion in front of the operations room, followed by two others. Sheets of flame leap up from the centre of a bunch of Beaufighters parked nearby and I am literally thrown on to my face on the ground by the blast.

This is the nearest I have ever been to a bomb and I am considerably shaken. For about five minutes I lay quivering on the ground watching three of our aircraft and a Flying Fortress burning furiously. I can see my machine "p" very near the flames but still looking quite intact. It is too near the fire to be safe and is right in the target area. I feel extremely annoyed about this and after a few minutes decide to try and move it. I run madly towards it and dope both the engines. I am shaken again as more bombs fall near the aerodrome and once more drop onto my stomach. Moments later I get up, climb into the cockpit and press the starter button. At first the engine turns over but will not start. I try the starboard one and it responds. I try the port one again and this time is starts - what a relief. I just push the throttle wide open and shoot off into the darkness at the south side of the aerodrome. I have never taxied an aircraft so quickly before.

When it is all over we go back into the operations room and an airman reports to the C.O. that there is a pilot laying on the runway who appears to be dead. He says that he is wearing a D.F.C. This shakes me because I know that the only D.F.C. pilot about was Hugh. We get a truck and go across the drome looking for him. I realise the worst. It is Hugh.

We find him laying near one of the burning Beaufighters with a shrapnel wound in his head. He must have been dead for over an hour. I give a hand to lift him on to the lorry.

We have only two aircraft left serviceable and I sleep in the Ops room for the rest of the night on readiness for one of them. Next morning I go out and look at the damage. Three Beaufighters and a Flying fortress have been burned out and about six other beaus damaged by shrapnel. Even "p" which I thought was alright has a piece of shrapnel through its port engine and several holes in the wings and fuselage.

Apparently Hugh's operator, Johnny Willlins, was also near the machine (as they were running to take off in it) and he was hit by a piece of metal in the arm. He was badly wounded and walked to the sick quarters. The Medical Officer said he was a very brave man. It will be several months before he can use his arm again so he will be sent back to England. A bomb also hit a main hangar in which some American Paratroops were sleeping. Twenty six of them were killed. Also the Flying Fortress had six people sleeping in it who were all killed.

I have no aircraft to service now so spend the day getting all Hugh's kit together and making an inventory of it, ready to go to his home. Everybody is pretty fed up about the night's bad luck and in the evening Johnnie Player, Tony and I go to Le Paris and have some wine. We have moved into the little Pub now and Tony and I share a room. It is quite comfortable here, particularly as Squadron Leader Elliot has managed to get some camp beds from the Air stores park. We also collect our own rations now and the landlady cooks them for us so this is a big improvement on the café.

22 November: Peter Dunning White turns up. He has had quite an uneventful trip by sea, in spite of the large number of U Boats known to be in the Straits. There is little to write about the next few days. I do not do any flying because of the shortage of aircraft. Most of my time is spent in helping to organise the mess and the two squadron offices we have acquired. On the 23rd and 24th there are small raids on the aerodrome and Algiers but little damage is done. On the evening of the 25th Tony and I go to Le Paris where we meet a hospitable Frenchman who invites us back to his flat. It is fourteen storeys up in a modern block of flats. We have a few drinks and stand on the balcony overlooking the docks. It is an exhilarating sight to see the moon shining on the water and the tall white buildings. While we are up there, the siren goes and several enemy aircraft drop bombs on the docks. It is an extraordinary sight too to see at one moment a beautifully peaceful city and the next a sky filled with flashes from gunfire as though some great, raging animal had been disturbed in its sleep.

We get back to the mess, Johnnie informs us that some pilots will have to go back to England the next day to collect new aircraft. I am extremely excited about this because it means I may have an opportunity to see Marie again for a day. There is lots of spinning of coins but the C.O. - bless him - gives priority to married people. I am very thrilled as I go to bed and I get up early to pack a few things the next morning.

26 November: The C.47 American paratroops transports are supposed to come from Oran to pick us up and take us to Gibraltar. It is not a very nice morning and we are rather doubtful whether they will arrive. They finally turn up at mid-day and we leave Maison Blanche at 2.30 pm. The weather is still not good and they are uncomfortable things to ride in so we are pleased when we arrive at Gibraltar three and a half hours later. Personnel coming back from Africa are allowed to go to a camp on the other side of the Rock known as the Governor's Lodge. This is a rest camp and we receive this privilege. It is very comfortable here and we get plenty of good food. Steak and chips are most welcome after the stew we have been living on lately.

At night Phil Kendall and I go to the cinema which is attached to the camp. Later I sleep well except for some disturbance from the blasting which is always going on here. Next morning, 27th November, I get up, have a warm salt water bath, a very good breakfast and go for a walk round Gibraltar. It is a beautiful day and Bob Griffiths and I go round the shops. I manage to get some exclusive perfume and silk stockings for Marie as well as some wines and sherries.

We have a good lunch, then go up to the aerodrome to see the transit officer. He informs us we shall be leaving for

England at midnight in another C.47. In the afternoon we go to the cinema in Gibraltar and after a few drinks go up to the aerodrome for dinner. I sleep in the mess until 11.30 pm and then take my gear out to the C.47. An American officer, Captain Smith, is flying us to England.

We take off just after midnight. It is a very lengthy trip because the C.47 will only cruise at about 160 miles per hour. So it takes nine hours to get to England. There are three of our squadron on this machine and a naval captain who has had his ship torpedoed. He is coming to England for a new commission. There is also a French army officer on board.

We talk and sleep and drink tea from our Thermos flasks and when it finally becomes light, we start looking out for the English coast. The visibility is very bad when we make a landfall and it takes the Navigator some time to find our position. We intended to land at Lyneham, near Swindon but because the weather is so bad, we go south and land at the first clear aerodrome we see which is Warmwell. After touching down I discover that the Whirlwind squadron is stationed here which Joe Holmes was in. I ring up and try to contact him but find that he was posted as a Flight Lieutenant to another squadron last week. There is a very nice mess in an old country house and we have an excellent lunch. After this we arrange with the Motor Transport section to let us have two vans to run us to Lyneham, It is about eighty miles and we get in at six o'clock. I have dinner and find my room and put a call through to Marie. She is very surprised and excited to speak to me so soon. It is marvellous to hear her voice again. I arrange to ring her the next day if I can get some leave.

29 November: The morning is spent at the stores getting new equipment and at lunch time Squadron Leader Elliot says we can all have a 48 hour pass. There is a rush for the Railway time table and we finish kitting up in record time. I share a taxi with Phil, Charlie Hill, Bob Griffiths and Kevin O'Sullivan to Swindon and have just time to put a call through to Marie to tell her that I arrive in Leeds at 2.30 am, before my train goes at 5.0 o'clock. Phil Kendall is going up to Leeds and Charlie Hill to Derby so we travel together. The train is late in but I am fortunate in getting a stray taxi up to Horsforth. I cannot describe the excitement of meeting Marie again and seeing Yvette and Suzanne.

30 November: When I wake up there is a disappointment for me. A wire has arrived ordering me to return the following morning which would mean I would have to leave |Leeds this afternoon. I am pretty annoyed about this and put in a call to Lyneham to see if I can alter it. Unfortunately, Johnnie Wright and Squadron Leader Elliot are not in the mess so I have to leave it and ring up later in the afternoon. I manage to catch Johnnie Wright this time and arrange with him that I should leave the following morning. The rest of the time at home goes far too quickly and I find myself kissing Marie goodbye again on the train in no time at all. It is surprising how often these farewells crop up.

I go to London, change at Paddington and have a snack on the station before catching my connection to Swindon. Also in the bar is Squadron Leader Elliot who has been home for the night so we travel back together. As it is quite late when we get to Lyneham, I have a meal and go to bed early.

2 December: I look at the new Beaufighter that I shall be flying out to North Africa. It is very similar to the old "p". We have to test it over the sea and fire its cannons and machine guns before it can be taken away. On the first trip, only one cannon goes off so we have to get the armourers to work on it. We take off in the afternoon and this time everything is in order.

3 December: I get up early, pack my things and go out with Charlie to swing our compasses. We have lunch and take off at 2.0 pm for Portreath, The weather is very bad and we have some difficulty locating it. Eventually Johnnie Wright and Sandow arrive and we all go along to the briefing room to work out our courses.

4 December: We are up at 4.0 am, have breakfast and go to the briefing room. I go out to run the engines up while Charlie takes account of the wind. When I return, the weather reports are very bad and the trip is washed out for the day. Johnnie, Sandow, Charlie and myself go into Redruth in the afternoon to a cinema.

5 December: The weather is still bad so we cannot take off. We play snooker in the morning and in the afternoon go to a cinema yet again.

6 December: We rise early at 3.30 am and I run my Beau up again. Apparently a Beaufort and some Hudsons are taking off at 5.00 am because the trip takes them longer than us. For some strange reason the Beaufort and a Hudson crash just after take off, killing all their crew. I see the flash where the Hudson hits the ground. I am also very shaken because, as the aerodrome is built on the cliff edge, my Beau, which I was running up at the time, is about fifty yards from the spot where the Beaufort hit the cliff. Apparently it took off, lost height over the sea and did a U turn into the cliff face. There was a colossal flash which lit up the aerodrome as his 600 gallons of petrol exploded. I have seen flashes as aircraft hit the ground before and it is not a pleasant sight.

After this I rather suspect sabotage and get my fitter and riggers to give my machine a good inspection. The Station C.O. is obviously perturbed by the incident and postpones our take off until daylight. We finally get airborne at 8.30 am. The weather is still not good over England (probably the reason for the crashes) but as we get across the Bay it improves considerably.

The trip is very similar to the last one with good weather over Portugal and we get into Gibraltar at about 2.15 pm. Johnnie Wright and Kevin O'Sullivan turn up later. Phil Kendall and Steve are supposed to have left but apparently turned back for some reason. I notice when going in to land that the battle ship Rodney is in the harbour. This is the ship that Howard Johnson, a friend from Leeds, is serving on so I decide to try and get in touch with him.

In the afternoon I walk round the town with Johnnie Wright and at five o'clock stroll over to the harbour to see if I can go aboard the Rodney. A liberty boat has just gone so I have to wait half an hour for the next one. It is the first time I have been on a battleship and I am impressed by its armour and size. I speak to the Officer of the day and he takes me to the ward rooms to see the Commander. He is a very good type of fellow and invites me to have some drinks. I am disappointed to learn, however, that Howard left the ship several months ago and has in fact left the service altogether. I find this very puzzling. I have several drinks and catch the next liberty boat back to the shore. Back at the mess I am just in time for dinner and after a few more drinks we turn in early.

7 December: Charlie and I load our aircraft and work out our course for Maison Blanche. It is a fine day and we set off at 10 o'clock. After a pleasant one and a half hour trip, we strike the African shore and from here onwards follow the coastline for another three hours. On landing, however, we find that most of the squadron has moved to an aerodrome near Bone.

We go down to the little pub for lunch where we meet Peter. He says that the aerodrome is about sixty miles from the front and that the boys have shot down quite a number of Huns. He says they are very short of pilots and planes and asks me to take another machine over after lunch that has already been fitted with equipment. However, Tony had tried to get there in the morning but returned later due to bad weather and problems with his radio.

I decide to fly along the coast where, if necessary, I can keep very low over the sea. As they are short of crews, it is agreed Tony and Hank Wall will come with me. We all load our kit, including camp beds into the Beaufighter and I take off with Tony, Hank and Charlie. It is rather an overload for a Beau - four people with full kit - but we get off alright. The weather deteriorates gradually and the cloud gets lower and lower until I am flying through rain at about 200 feet above the sea.

The aerodrome I am heading for is Souk el Arba which is sixty miles further on than Bone. It is well inland and surrounded by hills according to the map but although I can cope with flying low over the sea, it is going to be difficult getting over the 3000 feet mountains. When I arrive in Bone after one and a half hours, I am on the point of turning back when I see a clear patch ahead. This is fortunate because it enables me to scrape over the hills and down into the valley to Souk el Arba.

The country is remote and wild round here. There appear to be few French towns only Arab villages made up of mud huts. Souk el Aarba is a small, dirty place with a few French dwellings on it. When I fly over the aerodrome I can see two Spitfires burning on the ground. It is not an aerodrome as we know in England, just a piece of flat ground with no buildings at all. There are quite a number of Spitfires on the ground and I can see about four of our Beaus in one corner. After landing I taxi towards our planes where I find Cameron Cox and Jeff Humes, both "A" flight pilots. They tell me of the victories that everyone has been having. I am very pleased to hear that Johnnie Player has shot down a Heinkel III and two Italian Sovia Macceti's. The squadron score so far is eight. Mike Gloster had three, Cameron one and Jeff Humes two.

There is apparently no accommodation here apart from a nearby school which provides an Operations room and essential offices. Our squadron headquarters is a pile of petrol tins in the middle of the aerodrome with a field telephone amongst them. I meet Johnnie Player and he tells me that I shall be on the night flying programme. It has started to rain and the ground is getting extremely muddy making it difficult to drive the one and only 15 cwt Bedford lorry from the school across fields to the aerodrome.

Another squadron, 89, have a flight here and they put one flight on at night whilst we put on another. I know a pilot of their flight called Spurgin. He was in 68 squadron so he has many tales to tell. There is an improvised Cook house

71

in part of the school where we are able to get the usual stew, this having to be eaten standing up as there are no seats. The place is also very crowded with people clammering for food.

I am third off on the programme so I go back to the petrol tins and wait there in the rain by the telephone. Two people take off and return because the weather is bad. There are apparently no huns about. Johnnie Player brings the truck down and we huddle up in a corner of it out of the rain. It is very cold here at night. It seems to have been going on for ever when at 3.0 am the phone rings and Operations tell me to take off because they think there is a hun about. They think the weather is better at Bone but they have no Meteorological facilities. It is a very black night and I start up in the rain and taxi through the mud to the end of the flare path. The wheels sink deep as I open the throttles to take off and I am no sooner airborne than we run into solid cloud. This is very bumpy and instrument flying is a big strain as I know the place is surrounded by 3000 feet hills.

I keep on climbing and at 4000 feet, we start getting ice on our windscreen. As we get higher we hit an electric storm which makes sparks dance across and illuminate metal aerials and propellers like neon lights. It seems to get more bumpy as we get higher and we just hope that we will get out of it soon. It is finally 17,000 feet before the cloud thins out but still we have not emerged from the top so I try to keep to the lighter patches. I talk to Control and explain the position then decide to stay up above it. I can think of nothing more frightening than going down through that terrible blackness again in a country that is full of high mountains.

For four hours we continue dodging in and out of this dreadful cloud and hardly at any time do we manage to get our windscreens clear of ice in spite of the continual use of the de-icing pump. After another hour it is just getting light and we decide to fly well out to sea and come down. It is still very bumpy but fortunately the cloud has lifted about 2000 feet. It is with great relief that I catch sight of the sea again. In the early morning light, I have no trouble flying back to base down the valleys. Finally I land after one of the most frightening and strenuous trips I have ever had.

Next morning I put my camp bed in one of the school passages and try to get some sleep but this is very difficult with people continually walking past. For the next three days it rains continually. I am not on duty on the 8th December so Tony and I find a quieter place in the school to put our beds and so get a better night's sleep.

9 December: Squadron Leader Plessey, Commanding Officer of 89 Squadron, tells us he has found some billets in the village. We pack our kit on the Bedford and go round only to find some dirty Arab quarters with hundreds of bugs and rain pouring in through the roof. Some people put their beds up and try to sleep but I feel quite pleased that I am on readiness and do not have to spend the night there. Indeed, Freddie Lammer says he killed 250 bugs before settling down and that was after tipping two tins of Keetings on the floor.

I spend another very miserable night in the pouring rain in the back of the Bedford truck. The weather is too bad for the Hun so nobody takes off. It is incredible how long a night can be when you are wet and cold waiting in the rain next to a telephone.

10 December: It rains all day and as we are short of crews, I have to do readiness again. In the afternoon, I manage to give my aircraft a short test and knowing how miserable I was the night before, I decide to pack in my haversack a Thermos flask of hot tea, some chocolate and my pipe and tobacco. After this I always made a point of carrying these with me. On several occasions when I have been marooned in the middle of the aerodrome in pouring rain with the Bedford truck bogged in the mud, I have taken out my thermos flask, settled down on a petrol tin and had some hot tea and then lit my pipe. It is extraordinary how much this helped to improve the position and I was never quite as miserable again.

The night is very wet again but fortunately we have been able to get hold of a marquee. This is erected in the afternoon and we move our telephone into it although conditions are too bad for flying. The next morning we hear that Johnnie Player has found a new billet for us. It is the house of a wealthy Arab and is very clean. We move our beds into one of its large rooms and are just going to sleep when we hear aircraft overhead. A few minutes later there are two explosions as bombs explode near the station. They are two JU 88's taking advantage of the low cloud. Not long after they are back again and more bombs are dropped. The rest of the day is fairly quiet. At night I manage to get a cold bath and feel much better for it. The rain has stopped now and the clouds show signs of breaking.

12 December: Johnnie Player tells me that I have to run a General over to Bone for a conference this morning. I go and meet him at the Operations room and take him and a signals captain, who is also coming with us, out to the aeroplane. The General is a pleasant older man and is very impressed with the trip. We take off at 9.0 o'clock and I wait about half an hour at Bone whilst he talks to two other Generals. He returns at 11.0 and we fly back to Souk el Arba. He is very grateful for the time he has saved.

We are on readiness at night and are ordered to take off at 11.15. It is very dark but there are few clouds and the stars are bright. The ground is still muddy and the machine skids about as I race down the flare path. It is peculiar that Charlie expressed a hunch during the day that we should get our first Hun that night - and it came to be.

We climbed to 10,000 feet over Bone Bay. Towards the end of a raid, the controller gave us a course to steer after a bandit who had dropped his bombs and was making for home, presumably Sicily. He had rather a start on us and for about five minutes I had my Beaufighter full out indicating about 280 miles per hour. When corrected for height this is about 330 miles per hour. The Jerry was rapidly altering course in an effort to deceive night fighters. Several minutes later Charlie informed me that he had picked him up on his set and after changing course a few more times, I saw exhaust pipes about 1000 feet in front of us and above. I climbed up underneath these expecting returned fire from the rear gunner at any minute. It was not until I was 150 feet behind that I could definitely see that it was a Heinkel 111 by the width and dihedrial of its wings and its large tail. I was feeling very excited by this time and put my firing button to fire. I lifted the nose until the fuselage of the Hun was in the centre of my illuminated sight and for the first time in my life fired the guns at night.

There were great flashes in front of the aircraft as my cannons and machine guns went off which temporarily took away my night vision. After about two seconds, I stopped firing but could see no Hun in front of me and, for one fearful moment, thought I had missed him. This worry did not last long because I suddenly saw a flaming mass just below my starboard wing. I pulled to one side to get a better look and then realised the tremendous destructive power of my guns.

The fuselage of the Heinkel was burning furiously from stem to stern and I could see the conspicuous glass nose of the cockpit full of fire. The aircraft fell away with a vertical dive, leaving a string of sparks and burning debris behind it in the night sky. There was one large flash as it hit the sea and then no more. It was a horrible sight and the thought that it contained five men was foremost in my mind but overriding this was the knowledge that I had avenged Hugh's death and that these five men had set out on a mission to bomb our ships and kill our troops in Bone. It was our first Hun and Charlie and I simultaneously let out a rousing cheer. I informed Operations that we had bagged that bird and back came the usual RAF phrase "Good Show."

I forgot to mention that when I saw the machine again after shooting at it, I saw some brave person in the back fire at me. He missed by about fifty feet but it was extraordinary that any man in that flaming mass should attempt to fire back instead of trying to bail out. (Incidentally, there were no survivors).

When cannons go off they invariably give the Beau a good shaking up and it is not uncommon for a failure of some delicate instrument to follow. In this case it was our radio. Fortunately, we could just hear the controller enough to get a home bearing and had little difficulty finding our base and landing. We had a night flying supper and went to bed. I thought I may have some difficulty in sleeping but this was not the case. I slept solidly until 9.0 o'clock the next morning. Flight Sergeant Cameron had also got a Hun that night and 89 Squadron had got three. It shows the effectiveness of our night fighters when one realises that only six enemy aircraft attacked Bone that night and five of them were shot down.

The next day we received many congratulations from other chaps in the squadron and in the morning we went to the Intelligence officer and made out our combat report. Tony and I were walking back to our billet after lunch when we saw a snake. We had heard that there were some around here but this was the first one we had seen. It was about three feet long, a green colour and its two fanged tongue was darting in and out. We decided that it should be killed before it bit someone, so standing well clear because we did not know how fast it could move, we both aimed at it with our revolvers. Tony fired first, hitting it in the middle which made it very wild. I fired hitting it again but it took ten shots before it collapsed dead. We considered this a great feat and shot a line about it all day. Charlie and I were not on duty at night so we wrote letters and went to bed early.

14 December: We were awakened in the morning by bombs dropping in the village. It was another JU 88 going for the station. One of his bombs killed several soldiers but little damage was done to the station. I meet Johnnie Player at lunch time and he informs me that I am first off that night. It is a fine day and the aerodrome is drying up nicely now. It looks as if it should be a fine night too.

After tea Charlie and I go out to our aeroplane "V" and take off at about 6.15 pm just as it is getting dark. We patrol for about one and a half hours when the controller informs us that a raid is in the offing. We are sent after one Hun who (apparently being a wise bird) is rapidly changing course and height and also travelling at great speed. After a very hectic chase, we give this one up and are given a course for another Hun coming in towards Bone. After a few minutes Charlie picks him up on his set and we follow him through some S turns. Finally he straightened out and again I saw the telltale exhaust pipes.

The Jerry is now flying very steadily and as I look ahead I can see the reason for this. There are several flares over the Docks of Bone and this Hun is doing a run up to drop his bombs. There is also some flack coming up from the ships which is rather near to us. In a matter of seconds, I have identified it as another Heinkel 111 and have brought my illuminated gun sight into position on its fuselage. A short burst and the Jerry is burning as furiously as our first one. It went over onto its back and dived straight into the sea, ending as before in a large flash. It must have been a satisfying sight for the poor devils below to see the Hun crash down in flames in front of their ship. Another few seconds and he would undoubtedly have let his bombs go. As I watched this plane go down, I felt no pity for its crew and it was with the utmost satisfaction that we returned to base.

15 December: Johnnie Player has decided that, owing to the shortage of transport available for the squadron, it is necessary for us to live near the dispersal. Numerous tents are obtained and a camp is set up about 300 yards from our dispersal Marquee. We erect another Marquee for catering and about fifteen tents for sleeping purposes. Officers and air crew share four to a tent which is fairly comfortable. Mine includes Charlie, Cameron Cox and Peter Croft. We spend the rest of the day arranging our gear and go to bed at 8.0 o'clock.

16th December: I flew over to Bone to take Peter Dunning White to a meeting and bring the aircraft back to Souk el Arba. In the afternoon Charlie and I fly to Bone again to do our aircraft test and pick Peter up. Some Messershmitt 109's have been bombing the aerodrome a few minutes before we arrive and have shot a Hurricane down in the circuit. We meet the pilot walking back with a bullet in his arm. We wait about half an hour at Bone for Peter but he does not arrive so we have to go back to Souk as it is getting dark.

We are third on the programme so we wait in the dispersal Marquee whilst the first two go off. The night is suddenly disturbed by an aircraft which is obviously not a Beau. Charlie and I make a run for a trench and watch the dark shape flying low round the drome. The guns usually hold their fire as long as possible in these cases to avoid giving our position away. The Hun does a low run along the flare path and drops three bombs. After this all the guns open fire on him. He drops several more on the circuit, one quite near our tent and then goes away.

Johnnie Player drives down the flare path to see what damage has been done. Luckily the bombs have fallen clear of the runway so it is safe for further use. Operations ring up to say that one aircraft is having wireless trouble so it is returning to base and the other requires a relief. That means that Charlie and I must get airborne. We are rather shaken just as we get off the ground because the guns open fire on us. One shell actually hits the bottom of our fuselage and Charlie reports a small fire amongst the cannons. Luckily this goes out instantly and after an examination, Charlie confirms that there does not appear to be any damage. We get on patrol over Bone at 9.30 pm and stooge up and down for two hours without incident. Later however, Operations report that a raider is coming in so we are given a course to steer towards it. This appears to be an experienced pilot. (We learned later that it was a Pathfinder sent over to light the target up for the others.) Several minutes pass before Charlie picks him up and then we get in behind him. The Hun, apparently aware of our presence, goes into a dive, putting his wheels and flaps down and causing us to overshoot as he had reduced his speed to about 100 miles per hour. It is very difficult to fly a Beau as slow as this and, even with the use of our own wheels and flaps, it takes some time to slow down.

We call up Operations again and inform them that we have lost him so they give us another course to steer into him again. Charlie soon picks him up and after altering course and height violently several times we come up behind him once more. At about 1000 feet our speeds are synchronised at 180 miles per hour. I close in and see his exhaust pipes, obviously another Heinkel 111. Almost immediately the Hun throttles back again and puts his wheels and flaps down. This means that we are overshooting at great speed, probably doing about 40 miles per hour faster than the Hun and time does not permit the lowering of our own wheels and flaps. It is obvious that I must shoot immediately or lose the Hun for good as by this time he is running up on the harbour at Bone.

I open fire at a range much too close to be safe, about 75 feet, and almost immediately an enormous flash appears. My Beau flies straight through a colossal area of flames. It is the largest explosion I have ever seen. When we are in the darkness again, I am so dazzled that I cannot see any instruments or in fact anything at all and have a dreadful feeling that my aircraft must be on its back or diving.

In circumstances like these, I have learned to disregard my instincts so I decide to let the machine go its own way until I my vision returns. Suddenly I remember that Charlie has an air speed indicator in the back so I ask him if he can see it. I am very relieved when he says he can and that we are flying at the normal speed of 180 miles per hour. After what seems an age, I manage to focus on my instruments again and find that the aircraft is level but turning hard to starboard. I try to fly straight but nothing happens so I apply full opposite aileron which would normally make the machine turn hard the other way but it still continues to turn to starboard. This looks very serious. I stare at the windscreen and think for a moment that I am in cloud but soon discover that the whole of the front of the Beau is completely blackened by smoke. At this point, Charlie calls out that there is a strong smell of petrol so I examine the petrol gauges and find that the main starboard inner tank is empty, prompting me to change over to the other tank immediately. The position is very disturbing because I cannot see how the aircraft can possibly be landed so I call up Operations and report destroying the Hun. They must have seen it from the shore because the controller comments, "I'll say you got him." I request an emergency homing to the nearest aerodrome and inform him that I don't think the aircraft is landable and that we are going to bail out when we get over land.

It is easy enough to get the course to steer for Bone, which is the nearest aerodrome, but holding that course is a different matter because the Beau will not fly straight. For some time, by flying longer circles, I manage to get a little nearer to land and I tell Charlie to prepare to bail out. He opens his hatch and puts his parachute pack on ready to jump. The thing that worries me about this is that I know when I take my hand off the control column the machine will probably roll over onto its back, as it is requiring quite a lot of strength to keep it on an even keel.

After a while, I decide to try and clean a portion of my windscreen and manage, with some difficulty, to clear two small patches by putting my hand through the direct vision panel. It is a half moon night and being able to see out puts me much more at ease so I also decide to experiment with my engines. I find that by throttling the port motor back and opening up the starboard engine, the aircraft can just be flown straight with the use of full port aileron. In this way I manage to steer the course I have been given for Bone. This method meets with more success than expected so I tell Charlie that I will try and make a landing.

Parachute landings at night are always dangerous and often result in broken limbs or sprained ankles at the least. We also have to take into account that the country is very mountainous round here. I call up the controller and tell him of my decision and he says he will get every possible light on at Bone for me. The controller is Squadron Leader Brown and he is very helpful. He says, "Bail out if you have any doubts about it. It is you we want not the aeroplane."

I have made up my mind to try and land now so I continue to lose height. Charlie says he can see the floodlight some way behind so I manage to do a turn towards it. I do a very steep approach and, as soon as I see a runway, aim the machine straight for it. I had intended to land with my wheels up but as the position looks better than anticipated, I put them down at the last minute. The approach is very fast because I have to keep the starboard engine open to keep straight and I have to literally fly it at the ground. We touch the runway near the floodlight and I brake violently. I see a parked Spitfire on the side and miss it by about six inches. We overshoot the runway and hit a tent with the port wheel which collapses the undercarriage and swings the aircraft round. Charlie and I leap out of the top hatches and I am pleased to see that he is O.K. It is impossible to describe how good the earth feels after a trip like that.

Almost immediately, fire engines and ambulances dash up to us. They have apparently been standing by expecting the worst. We examine our aircraft and find that all the canvas is burned off the starboard aileron and some of the elevators. The machine is blackened all over with smoke and oil and the paintwork is badly blistered. The ambulance runs us to the Operations room where we get a good reception. The Duty Controller rings up a hotel in Bone which has been taken over by the RAF to get us a room and asks the cook to make us a hot meal. He also arranges for transport to take us there.

The Hotel St Cloud is situated right on the front of Bone Bay. The calm water lapping the sands looks very beautiful as we drive up. It is so quiet and peaceful here that it is difficult to connect it to the fiery battle we had 10,000 feet above less than an hour before. I am pleased to get to bed and have no trouble going to sleep as I feel completely exhausted. The strain of those minutes before the kill was very great even though I did not notice it all the time.

Next morning I am awake quite early and do not feel like sleeping again so I get dressed and have a stroll along the sands. It is very refreshing. When walking back to the hotel I saw Peter standing outside who had apparently spent the night there too. I told him our story and he says he has borrowed a van to drive back to Souk el Arba. I am pleased about this chance to get a lift so I go in to tell Charlie and we all set off together for Souk. On the way we pass near Bone aerodrome so call in to look at our Beau in daylight.

It has suffered more from the explosion than I had realised the night before. All the paintwork is blistered and any wooden parts are charred and burned. The aileron is reduced to a frame with no canvas on it at all and a piece is missing out of the elevator. Peter is astounded that the thing was flyable at all. I realise that we were extremely lucky that our own tanks did not explode with the heat.

The drive back to Souk el Arba is very pleasant. The scenery on the hills is attractive and reminds me of Scotland. It is a beautiful day and I am pleased to have had the chance of doing this drive. We arrive in Souk around lunchtime and tell our story to all. In the afternoon Charlie and I make out our intelligence report and then go to bed early.

18 December is a wet day. It clears for an hour in the afternoon and we manage to do a night flying test. We are on the programme but it rains continually so we sleep at dispersal and are not disturbed.

19 December is uneventful. We are not on duty and most of the day is spent writing and reading.

20 December is a fine day. We do a night flying test in the afternoon and at tea time are disturbed by a Focke Wulf 190. Charlie and I are eating in the marquee when the guns go off. Everybody rushes for the trench and as I leave I can see four Focke Wulf 190's flying very low across the aerodrome, firing their guns and cannons. As I run I get a glimpse of a bomb leaving the first machine. They all drop bombs on the aerodrome but apart from minor shrapnel damage to two of our aircraft we suffer no further damage

We are on the programme at night and are ordered to take to the air at 7.30 pm. It is a full moon night and it looks as bright as day. The Controller tells us that some Huns are coming over at 18,000 feet. This is rather high for a Beau but we get up there and steer varying courses after a Jerry. It is hard work changing course rapidly at this altitude because the Beau is very sluggish to the controls and it is difficult to maintain height. After about ten minutes of this we are told that there is a Hun at about 12,000 feet so we lose height fast and after several minutes Charlie reports that he has picked him up. Rather an erratic chase follows and finally I see the Hun silhouetted against a cloud. It is a clear shape and obviously another Heinkel 111.

This time I am determined not to get too close so I manoeuvre behind him at about 120 feet. It is very bright and I am expecting the rear gunner to take a pot at me any minute because I must have shown up very clearly against the white clouds behind. For the fourth time I pull my sights up onto the fuselage of the Heinkel 111 and press the button. The result is not satisfying. Only one cannon fires a single round and my machine guns are making an unusual chug chugging noise. I hold the sights on for several seconds but the Hun looks quite intact and no flames are visible.

After this the Jerry goes into a steep dive which increases his speed so, not intending to lose him, I open up to full throttle and follow him, gradually getting closer. I keep my sights on him all the time with great difficulty and fire the remainder of my machine gun ammunition. At the end of this time we are both travelling very fast in a steep dive and as we get to 5,000 feet I draw alongside him. The Hun is still not burning but continues in the steep dive. There is some cloud at 4,000 feet so I pull out and the Hun goes through it. We are not at all satisfied that we have destroyed this one so I call up Operations and tell them about it. A few minutes later we are very relieved when they call us up and tell us that the hostile aircraft definitely hit the ground. I think my machine gun fire must have killed the pilot and gunners. Having used all my ammunition, we return to base. This brings our score to four which makes us the Aces of the Squadron, the next highest being Johnnie Player with three.

21 December is very uneventful. We are not on readiness and do no flying.

22 December: We have more visits from enemy aircraft. Just after breakfast a Focke Wulf 190 flies over the aerodrome. It does not drop any bombs or fire its guns so we assume the crew must have been taking photographs. Later in the morning a JU 88 flies over very low, also not dropping bombs. This rather makes us think that a heavy raid is in the offing so we decide to dig our trench a little deeper. The arrangements of the tents has been altered slightly so that now Charlie and I share one with Pilot Officer Stephen and Flight Sergeant Wood, his operator. We have previously spent quite a lot of time digging a trench near our tent to take the four of us but there is room for plenty of improvement.

I forgot to mention that last night 89 Squadron lost one of its most valuable pilots, Flight Lieutenant Mitchell. He was a charming type of man and liked by everybody. Apparently he had some trouble with his Beau and tried to crash land at Bone. He must have stalled turning in because both he and his operator were killed instantly.

22 December: In the morning Peter asks me to go over to Bone with him to bring his aeroplane back. We set off but when we get near, the weather is so bad that we have to return. We have some difficulty finding Base again and when we do find out where we are, it is a little too close to enemy lines for comfort. The weather is a little better in the afternoon so Charlie and I do a night flying test.

By nightfall the weather is not good but, as there are Huns about, we take off at 9.30 pm. In fact there are very few and what there are appear to be flying low down, looking for shipping rather than going for Bone. For about an hour we fly at 1000 feet above the sea. It is very unpleasant as there are many rain and thunderstorms in the clouds and 1000 feet is rather too low to be comfortable in these conditions.

We have no success and the Huns go home again so we climb higher. Operations have had a message that the weather is closing at Base so we make for home. We try and climb above cloud to cross the mountains and it is 14000 feet before we emerge from them. Fortunately there is a hole in the clouds near Base so we go through it and land. There is no more flying during the night because it starts to rain and there is no further enemy activity.

23 December: It rains all day. I learn from someone that there are special facilities for sending wires home at Christmas at the Army Post Office in Souk el Arba so Charlie and I take the Bedford van and go in with Ron Winsor. I manage to send a wire to Marie and also one to Mother and Dad, Mrs Garner and Ruth and Pat. We drive round the village trying to buy wine etc. for Christmas. Nothing further of interest happens on the 23rd.

24 December: It rains hard all day yet again. In the afternoon we manage to get an aircraft test in as we are on duty at night. By the evening, however, the ground is so boggy that the Group Captain will only allow flying in case of emergency so we do not patrol. It continues to rain and the sky looks leaden so we sleep at Dispersal all night.

25 December: The Group Captain informs the Wing Commander that he has heard the Hun is massing aircraft, presumably to try and destroy the RAF on the ground. He thinks it is likely we shall have a heavy raid. So once again we improve our trench and fill petrol tins with earth to place strategically around it. We have had some bottles of whisky and gin sent so we have a few drinks on Christmas morning.

The rain does not let up and at two o'clock we go across to a barn where it has been decided to have our Christmas dinner. The meal is an excellent effort. Ron Winsor has managed to buy a pig and some turkeys and the catering staff have made a very good job of the cooking. Everybody thoroughly enjoys it and there is plenty of wine flowing. Toasts are drunk to the King, the Wing Commander and Johnnie Player and even I have the honour of having to say a few words as the pilot with the highest score to date.

Most people are feeling rather tight after dinner and there is much singing. It is amusing to see the old Arabs looking on. When the Village Chief appears we give him a chair and a mug of wine and he is very honoured though it is fortunate he cannot understand the rude things that are said to him.

After several contests at riding Arab donkeys, we go back to our tents at about 4.0 o'clock and sleep until evening. The Wing Commander had intended to have a sing song later but everybody is much too tight to turn up for it. Luckily the aerodrome is still too boggy to fly so nobody has to venture into the sky that night although the people on readiness say that they could have done so if necessary.

26 December: Boxing Day is still wet and cold so in the morning we remain in our tent except for running down to the cookhouse marquee to collect our breakfast. Lately, we have had numerous Arabs coming round selling eggs which make a very welcome change. The cooks are very hard working, helpful sort of chaps and always oblige by frying them for us when we take them down to breakfast.

Johnnie Player and Wing Commander Kelly go by car to Setif in the afternoon, leaving me in command of "B" Flight. I should mention here that as this Base is very forward and within easy reach of enemy fighters and bombers, it was decided that only the bare minimum of aircraft and aircrews should be kept up here to do nightly readiness. A Base some 200 miles back has been formed at Setif where aircraft are kept and maintained and where aircrews can go for a rest after about a fortnight while relief crews are sent down to take their place. Charlie and I are due to go there for a break any day now and would in fact have gone before if weather conditions at Setif had permitted a relief to be sent.

In the afternoon, Charlie and I manage a night flying test but the surface of the aerodrome is very boggy and dangerous. At night several people go after Huns which do not arrive and at 4.0 o'clock in the morning I get ordered to take off because several bandits have appeared well out to sea. Unfortunately my starboard engine refuses to start so I tell Pilot Officer Stephen to go instead. It seems that the Huns are not going for Bone but for a convoy at sea. Steve flies round the vicinity for quite a while only to be shot at by the Navy so he returns to Base. He says the weather was bad out there and he was in cloud all the time.

Unfortunately, being Flight Commander means that it is not possible to get any sleep during the night so I am very tired when dawn breaks. Steve lands in the early morning and gets his aircraft bogged down taxiing back and, before it can be moved, a careless Spitfire pilot hits one of its propellers and rudder taking off. Fortunately, the Spit got away with it but it will put another of our valuable aeroplanes out of action for some time.

27 December: I go to bed after breakfast and sleep until lunch time. In the afternoon I supervise the putting out of the Flare path and the evening is spent writing to Marie and updating this Diary. At 8.0 o'clock we borrow a Primus stove from the next tent and fry some eggs. We have got a newcomer to our tent today, that is Crackers, or Flight Officer Cracknell, the Squadron Intelligence Officer. He has just arrived by rail from Setif after about a twenty four hour journey and has plenty of hard work to do catching up with all our combat reports.

28 December: At last a fine day and the aerodrome shows every prospect of drying up. In the afternoon, Charlie and I go up on a night flying test. We have got our old Beau "p" back again. Jeff Humes brought it over from Setif yesterday where it had gone for repairs following the wounds it received at Maison Blanch. We have to land again owing to our transmitter being unserviceable and I am just taxiing along the side of the runway when a Beaufighter comes in to land with its wheels up. I am most annoyed that I cannot transmit because, had I been able to, I could easily have warned the pilot in time to save the machine. As this was impossible, the Beau held off along the runway and then dropped onto its two engines, smashing its propellers before swinging round on the port wing.

I taxied in and was very sorry to learn that it was Steve. Luckily both he and his operator were alright apart from shock. Steve frankly admitted that he had just forgotten to put his wheels down. He is quite an experienced pilot but it is extraordinary how the most competent airmen can forget the most elementary things.

We are third on the programme at night but as the first two machines are not serviceable, we go off at dusk. After three and a half hours patrolling with no chases we return to base and come in to land. Unfortunately as we touch down our port tyre bursts and we swing violently off the runway into the darkness. I am sure that we are going to hit one of the many Spitfires parked on the aerodrome at any minute but fate is good to us and after doing a circle we come to a standstill, the only damage being our burst port tyre. We walk back to the dispersal and Charlie complains that his tummy is giving him trouble so, as we have no serviceable aeroplane, we decide to turn in.

29 December: In the morning we pack ready to go to Setif and put our kit in aircraft "R." This machine has to go there to have its undercarriage repaired as it has been sprained and is not safe to retract. We are therefore obliged to fly it to Setif with its undercarriage down. "R" is a notably unstable aeroplane under the best of conditions but its maximum speed with wheels down is only 130 miles per hour. It is extremely hard work keeping it on an even keel, in fact it takes us an hour to climb to the 6,000 feet necessary to get over the high mountains. After two hours we arrive at Setif aerodrome which is 3,600 feet above sea level and right in the midst of these peaks.

This is an excellent place for a rest camp. The air is simply terrific and the snow capped mountains surrounding us are a very beautiful sight. Our living quarters are five miles from the aerodrome and again consist of tents but as it is only necessary to have two officers to a tent and we have our batmen here, conditions are much more comfortable than

Souk.   We have an Officers mess in a house near the tents with a warm wood fire which is extremely welcome as it is quite cold up here. Dinner at night is a pleasant surprise. We have soup, fresh meat, potatoes and carrots, extremely well cooked, and a sweet, cheese biscuits and coffee.   One can imagine what my reactions to these are after living on stew for several weeks. We also have a good radio here and at 9.0 o'clock we have the English news. This is the first news that can be relied on that I have heard for weeks.

30 December: I have a good night's rest and wake up the next morning to find the ground white with frost. It is good to have the batman bring some hot water and in spite of the cold I feel extremely fit. At the mess I find a good helping of bacon and eggs waiting for me and after breakfast went for a four mile walk.   Apparently, apart from Orderly office duties once a week, we have no other duties here so it will be a complete rest. The afternoon is spent writing. At night I have some drinks in the mess and a round of Pontoon.

31st December: I go for another walk in the morning with Ron Winsor. In the afternoon we go into Setif to look around. It is quite a small town but we manage to buy some odd things. Later we go to the Café Pepiniere for a drink. The Bedford van picks us up at 7.30 pm and we go back to the mess for dinner. Being New Year's Eve we have quite a lot of wine accompanied by song. The C.O. pays off his debts in bottles of wine and since he has promised them to anyone successful in destroying a Hun, I touch him for four. We end the evening by going for a sing song in the Sergeants mess, let the New Year in and turn in about 1 o'clock.

1 January: Ground again white with frost. Very cold but a beautiful day. The thing I like about this place is that we do not get hundreds of infernal insects and beetles up here. I suppose it is too cold for them. There has been rather a flap for the last two days because an enemy troop carrying glider has landed near the aerodrome but none of its occupants have been found. During the night, three more gliders landed but fortunately all the troops from them were captured.

Last night a drunken Corporal knocked a lamp over and set the Cook House tent on fire. In the afternoon Jeff Humes arrives from Souk el Arba with a story that Arthur Woolley knocked a lamp over and burned a tent. Jeff only just got out of his bed in time but he lost all his clothes and equipment. Apparently yesterday there was another raid on Souk and a JU 88 got a direct hit on Aircraft V8519 (the second one I collected from England) also bits of shrapnel damaged "p" again so the one bomb damaged and destroyed both the aircraft that I had brought out. Poor old "p" has only just been repaired from its wounds received in Maison Blanch and now it has more holes in it.

In the afternoon, I go into Setif with Ronnie and have a bath. At night two French Army officers run us back to the camp. They come into the mess for a drink. They say that five more German glider troops have been captured near the aerodrome.

2 January: Saturday. Frosty morning again. I have some tummy trouble. Everyone seems to have a touch of it and it usually last two days. I turn in early. A new pilot replacement for Hugh arrives, Pilot Officer Spawl or Gordon.

3 January: Sunday. Nothing of much interest. My tummy is feeling better. In the evening I play Poker with Peter, Johnnie Player, Ron and Cobber. Go to bed at 11.0 o'clock. Cameron Cox moves into my tent. The news comes through at night that Johnnie Wright shot down a Dornier 217 last night but there seems to be some argument as to whether it was a 217 or an Italian Breda 20. This brings the Squadron score to 17 destroyed and one damaged in North Africa.

4 January: Monday. Spend the morning writing in the mess. Nothing more of interest. It is over a week since I have flown now and I do not intend to fly until I go back to Souk again. I am feeling much better for the rest. It is strange that one never realises what a strain flying is until you stop for a few days. The constant threat of bombing at Souk keeps you always on the alert and in consequence a night off at Souk is not really a rest.

5 January: Tuesday. Very uneventful day. Lose at Poker at night.

6 January: Wednesday. Decide to go to Constantine with Ron Winsor. We get a lift with three Officers from the Air Ministry in a Bedford. It is ninety miles and rather a monotonous trip. Constantine, however, is a beautiful town - not as large as Algiers but a cleaner place. We find a hospital that has been converted into an RAF hotel and fix some beds for the evening. At lunchtime we go to Casino Bar. It is very crowded with pilots back from the front for a rest. I meet several officers from 152 Squadron that I met at Souk flying Spitfires. We drink and chat about the scraps we have had and finally leave the bar at 3.30 pm rather the worse for wear. At night we have dinner at the Hotel de France and go back to the hospital. There is a bar in the Mess and we meet the few remaining crews from 18 Squadron Bisleys. They have had very bad luck and lost most of their pilots. These boys think they will be going back to England to reform.

7th January: Thursday. Up at 9.0 o'clock. We have a look round the shops and get a lift back to Setif in a French officer's car. We arrive back at the Mess in time for lunch and are greeted with some good and bad news. The good news is that Johnnie Player and his Operator Freddie Lamer, and Mike Gloster and his Operator Pilot Officer Oswald have each been awarded a D.F.C. I am pleased Johnnie has got one. He certainly deserves it. The bad news is that Flying Officer Weston and Pilot Officer Hiles were killed last night at Souk el Arba when their engine caught fire. They crashed trying to land at Bone. I spend all the afternoon censoring a heap of letters from airmen.

8 January: Friday. We have to leave for Souk el Arba today so I go into Setif in the morning to collect my washing etc. Charlie and I take off at 2.30 pm and have quite a pleasant trip to Souk. We are not on duty at night so we get our kit fixed up in a tent with Phil Kendall and Charlie Hill. They are both very excited because they shot an Italian Cant down last night.

Just as I was taxiing out at Setif, an airman ran out and gave me a letter from Marie. This is a marvellous surprise and is the first one I have had since I left her at Leeds station.

9 January: Saturday. Charlie and I are on the programme at night so we do a test in the afternoon. We are the last on the list and, as the weather closes in around midnight, we return to our tent and go to bed.

10 January: Sunday. Nothing of interest to write. It rains continually all day and the aerodrome gets very boggy. In the afternoon I supervise the laying of the Flare Path. At night I write and Charlie and I cook omelettes.

11 January: Monday. Censor letters in the morning. Do a night flying test in the afternoon and take off on patrol at dusk. There is bad icing on the wings and it is very unpleasant because we are flying in cloud most of the time. The weather has deteriorated a lot when we return to Base after two and a half hours and, as there are no Huns about, I am pleased to get down. We have some supper and go back to our tent to bed. Nobody else flies during the night.

12 January: Tuesday. The aerodrome is drying up and it looks like being a better day. Phil has tummy trouble and stays in bed in the morning. I spend the morning censoring letters. Not on at night so do not do a test. At tea time we are disturbed by Ack Ack, grab our tin hats and make for the trench. We see about three JU 88's fly over the aerodrome at a high altitude with the flack bursting all round them. They drop their bombs but they all miss the aerodrome.

More JU 88's keep on coming over until dark but all the bombs are wide. At night Cameron Cox and Freddie Lammer come to have a drink in our tent. At 10.0 o'clock a very bad thunder storm crops up and continues through most of the night. The lightening is the worst I have ever seen and the wind is terrific. Several times during the night we thought we had lost our tent but luckily it stood up to it.

13 January: Wednesday. The wind has abated but the ground is more boggy than ever after the torrential rain. During the morning we are disturbed by two Focke Wulf 190's machine gunning the local village. All the Ack Ack guns open up on them as they make for their own lines again. Later whilst I am censoring letters, I hear aircraft diving over the drome and, as I run for our trench, see that it is three Messershmitt 109's. They come low and machine gun the

96

aerodrome. We hear later that the A.A. guns have accounted for one of them.

We were on the programme but the aerodrome is too boggy to do a night flying test. We are last on the list but after dark the weather improves so we decide to do a standing patrol. Charlie and I take off at 2.0 o'clock and circle for three and a half hours but there are no Huns about.

14 January: Thursday. Sleep until 11.0 am and then cook our own breakfast. At 11.30 Cameron Cox and Peter come in for a gin. Have a bath in the afternoon. It is the first time I have tried out my camp kit bath and it is quite a success. It is a beautiful day so I sunbathe all afternoon.

15 January: Friday. On the programme at night so do usual flying test. I am second off and am scrambled at 9.15 pm. I have a long chase after a Hun at 12.000 feet but do not get a contact. The enemy aircraft just flies round our base and returns to Sicily again. It does not drop any bombs. Fly for two hours and then land. Phil Kendall takes off later and shoots a Cant 1007 down at 20,000 feet. Charlie and I go back to our tent to sleep.

16 January: Saturday. Sleep in the morning and in the afternoon go fishing in the local river with Phil and Charlie Hill. Catch one fish. At night go for a drink in Cameron's tent.

17 January: Sunday. It is a beautiful day. Have a gin with Cameron and Peter in the morning. Last night Peter crashed his Beau whilst landing but both he and Cobber are alright but Peter is upset about the Beau. We have now only eight Beaufighters left and can only get four serviceable for night flying. Hugh Elliott and Cameron Cox have to go and operate from an aerodrome near Bone at night so Phil and I are the only two people on readiness here. Both our machines are having jobs done on them so we are unable to do night flying tests. I take off at dusk and patrol for three and a half hours but apart from chasing two unidentified aircraft, which disappeared when we got near them, we have no further chases.

18 January: Monday. Sleep all morning. Learn that we have got three new crews from England at Setif with three new aircraft. This will relieve the position considerably. At night we go for a drink in Cameron's tent. Mike Gloster shoots down another Italian Cant 1007 bringing the Squadron score to 20 in North Africa.

19 January: Tuesday. Phil Kendall and I have to go over to Tingley aerodrome near Bone to operate at night. It has been decided that we could get off the ground quicker here to intercept Bone raids and so avoid patrolling all night. It is a nice afternoon and we take off from Souk el Arba at about 2.30 pm so that we can do an air test on the way.

Tingley has a very nice steel runway but it is rather short for Beaus and also it has a 2000 foot hill about four miles away. This makes it dangerous for night flying. It is therefore agreed that we shall only take off from here and land at Souk. I have some difficulty getting a Flare Path organised with Hurricane lamps and petrol tins similar to the one at Souk. We have tea and settle ourselves down in a Marquee with a telephone. Having spun a coin for position, Phil is first off. We play cards until 10.0 o'clock when the phone rings for one aircraft to scramble so Phil goes off. Unfortunately, it is a false alarm because the bandits turn out to be Bisleys returning from a raid on Tunis. Phil patrols for two hours and returns to Souk.

Charlie and I try and sleep on the floor until about 4.0 o'clock when we get fed up and decide to patrol, so we speak to Operations and take off. We patrol over Bone Bay for an hour with no excitement but at 5.10 am Operations call me up and inform me that there is an unidentified aircraft well out in the Mediterranean, very high up, so we steer an easterly course towards it and climb. After a few minutes, they tell us to continue climbing to 20,000 feet. A Beau is very sluggish at heights like this and the rate of climb gets very slow after 15,000 feet. Also, as I have got the engines full out, the oil and engine temperatures are getting disturbingly high. When we finally arrive at 20,000, we are still flat out and on varying courses. I am very shaken when suddenly all my instruments appear to go red and things in the cockpit begin to swim about. My head too feels heavy and I find it difficult to think clearly. It is because of this that it takes me some time to work out the problem which is, of course, lack of oxygen. As soon as I realise this, I feel down the tube from my helmet and follow it to the plug in the cockpit, where I find that it is not plugged into the cockpit properly. I push this in again and turn the oxygen indicator up to 35,000 feet and slowly come back to my senses again. Charlie has been wondering what the devil was wrong with my flying.

After some time at this height, Charlie gets a contact and we have to go up another 1,000 feet to get behind the aircraft, making us 21,000 feet. We are fairly close I am able to see exhaust pipes in front of me because my vision is still not back to normal and it takes me quite some time to realise that it is a three engined machine in front which obviously earmarks it as Italian.

I close into range and, identifying it as a Cant 1007, bring my sights onto its slim fuselage. I press the button only to find that my cannons are not firing, just my wing machine guns. It is fortunate that some bullets hit their mark. I can see them sparkle as they strike the wings and body of the Cant. Almost immediately, the enemy peels away into a spiral dive in an endeavour to shake me off but my shooting has winged him and I can see his port motor burning as he dives down. I peel off into a dive myself, with my Beau full out and call to Charlie to recock the guns. He has some difficulty doing this because when he releases his straps, he gets thrown about the back. At about 14,000 feet Charlie informs me that he has recocked so I pull to the inside of the spiral and take another deflection shot at him. Again only the machine guns fire and no decisive results follow. Once more I call to Charlie to recock. I am now diving at about 380 miles per hour, spiralling straight down after the Cant and having great difficulty in keeping below the level of his tail. I know that Cants have a pretty formidable top gun position so I do not intend to become a target for this man. At 8,000 feet, Charlie says O.K. again and I take another deflection shot at him. This time two cannons go off and straight away the other two engines and starboard wing start burning. I pull out of the dive at 6,000 feet and the blazing Cant continues to plunge through the cloud layer which is at about 5,000 feet. We do an orbit above the cloud and see a large flash followed by a red glow showing through. I call up Operations again and tell them about it. They are rather alarmed at me getting too far east. They ask me to return to the Bone area as quickly as possible because they have another bogy for me. I return and chase their plots inland but we are unable to get a contact and they finally tell me they think it is a friendly.

Having had two occasions when cannons failed I took the matter up with the armaments officer. He said the reason for this was the very low temperature at 20,000 feet, often in excess of minus ten degrees, which made the oil stiff round the Brevil blocks. I don't think they had been fired at this height before.

We return to Souk el Arba to find that there is a nasty ground mist so decide to stay up for another half hour until dawn. The weather is still pretty bad but after some difficulty we manage to make a safe landing.

20 January: Wednesday. Stay in bed all morning. The Intelligence Officer comes to see us so we give him the report over a bottle of gin. Receive a letter from Marie.

21 January: Thursday. The Wing Commander arrives from Setif with Gordon, the new pilot, and, as they are flying, we have the night off. Phil Kendall and Charlie Hill fly back to Setif for a rest. Pilot Officer Phillips gets a Heinkel 111.

22 January: Friday. Go over to Tingley again in the afternoon with Mike Gloster. We have tea there and lay the Flare Path. I am first off and am scrambled at 8.0 o'clock. We get over Bone area and chase several Huns but unfortunately they are flying too low for us to be effective. Peter Dunning White chases one back to its base in Sardinia but is unable to catch it up. We pursue odd aircraft for three and a half hours and then return to Souk el Arba.

23 January: Saturday. Sleep until 11.0 o'clock. We are not on duty at night so spend the afternoon writing. Hear the news that Tripoli has fallen which is a good show.

Several Messershmitt 109's fly over in the morning but they do not attack us. Several sweeps of our Flying Fortresses go over to bomb Tunis. We can hear the bombing here at Souk. Also at night we can hear some heavy artillery.

It sounds as if the boys are making a push. At 10.0 o'clock an enemy aircraft flies over and drops fourteen light bombs on the aerodrome. Fortunately no damage is done.

24 January: Sunday. Go to a church service on the camp in the morning. Test "p" in the afternoon. Two new crews have arrived. I am second off at night but the weather is not good and there are no hostiles about so I sleep at dispersal. Get some souvenirs of my Cant sent along.

25 January: Monday. Sleep until 11.0 o'clock. An R.A.F. press man arrives and wants the story of our victories. He takes two photographs of Charlie and I. We are not on duty at night so go to Peter's tent to play Poker. Wind up with the usual omelettes. It is another bad night and there is no flying. Hear the 9.0 o'clock news. It is very good. Gerry retreating on all fronts. Another new crew arrives.

26 January: Tuesday. Another wet morning. The weather improves towards midday and at lunch time another incident occurs which spells 26th January as a black day for the Squadron. Charlie and I have just finished lunch when we hear a screaming noise. I go outside and look into the air (now a beautiful day) and cannot see anything. The scream increases in intensity closely followed by a loud explosion. Charlie and I do not have time to run to the trenches so we fall flat on our stomachs on the ground. This episode is followed by another steadily increasing scream and a further explosion nearer than the last one. We are both rather shaken because the noise is terrific and the whole earth seems to vibrate. I quickly realise that we are being dive bombed and that the Huns are coming straight out of the sun, making it impossible for us to see them. Four more screaming attacks and explosions follow and the suspense after each one is sickening, just waiting for the bomb to land, particularly as they all appear to be getting nearer. The last bomb is the most unnerving of all. It lands about thirty yards away from us and we can hear little bits of shrapnel landing all around us. After it is all over we stand up and Charlie picks up two pieces of jagged metal that have landed a few feet away from us.

We look towards the last crater which is near the cook-house and see a mutilated cow lying on the ground. At first I thought it was a human. At the aerodrome a column of black smoke is rising from one of our Beaus. I go across with Peter and Cameron to examine the damage and we find that two Beaus have been completely written off and all the others holed with shrapnel. Also an unfortunate armourer was near the Beaus and he was literally blown to bits. This has completely upset our service for the evening and once again there is a great depression over the camp.

By the evening, we have only managed to get one Beau serviceable and that is "R" which actually had five holes in it but fortunately they caused no structural damage and could all be covered over. As I am the first on the programme, I stand by in this machine. Everything is quiet until 4.0 o'clock in the morning when I am scrambled for some hostile aircraft approaching base. We get off the ground in record time which is just as well as a few minutes later one of the enemy planes drops about a dozen incendiary bombs down the Flare Path. We spend two and a half hours chasing these hostiles about but both the weather and the controlling is bad so our efforts are in vain. At dawn we return to Base and land with no success.

27 January: Wednesday. Sleep all morning. It is a wet day. In the evening Peter, Cameron, Jeff and I have been invited to a Mess at Souk el Chermis for a drink so we go along in the 15 cwt Bedford. When we arrive, we find that it is old farm that has been converted into a bar and the effect is very good. The oak bar itself has been made out of an old wardrobe and high stools made from round bomb fin cases. Also on the walls are drawn rather clever cartoons of Pilot Officer Prune, Hitler and rather skimpily dressed ladies.

Group Captain Lees is here and is in excellent form. We have several sing songs and the boys of the Hurricane Bomber Squadron prove to be a very good crowd. I shall always remember the way they picked up their tin stools and beat them like native drums while the Group Captain did a war dance in the centre. The party went on until 1.30 am when we made our way home again all slightly the worse for wear.

28 January: Thursday. Peter told me that I am due to return to Setif, so Charlie and I pack all our kit into "R" ready to depart. We are held up for an hour because the C.O. decides to fly back with us. I take off at 2 o'clock and have quite an uneventful journey. It is very pleasant to have a bath again and put on some clean clothes.

29 January: Saturday. What a treat to have a batman bring me hot shaving water. In the mess I am greeted with the news or rather rumour that Marshall law has been declared in Germany. If this is true, the end must be getting near and everyone feels very optimistic about the outcome. I go into Setif in the afternoon and do a little shopping. Practically all the things worth buying there have been bought and the shops look empty. We have a few drinks in the mess at night and go to bed early.

30 January: Saturday. Nothing of interest to report. It is a beautiful day. I go into Setif again with Bob Griffiths for a haircut and we have lunch at the Hotel Le France.

31ˢᵗ January: Sunday. Cameron Cox arrives and shares my tent. We have some drinks at night and later go to the Sergeants Mess.

1ˢᵗ February: Monday. I go to the Intelligence Room in the morning with Cameron and confirm the suspicion I have had for some time now that my fourth victory was not a Heinkel 111 but a Fiat B.R. 20. This crashed six miles from Bone on 20ᵗʰ December. I get onto Eastern Air Command and confirm that I was officially credited with this. Cameron and I sunbathe all afternoon and turn in early at night. The C.O. returns from Souk el Arba. He says that all our Squadron will be moving back here and 600 Squadron taking our place at Souk.

2 February: Tuesday. The C.O. says Cameron and I can take 10 days leave so we pack a case and hop on to a lorry going to Algiers. It is about 180 miles and after the first 60 miles we find it very uncomfortable and slow so we stop an RAF Humber Snipe. The driver turns out to be our old friend the engineering officer from Maison Blanch. It is a very mountainous road with excellent scenery. We get to Maison Blanch just after dark and the engineering officer kindly invites us to stay the night. We have dinner at their new mess, a very nice old French house which they have taken over.

3 February: Wednesday. I go up to Maison Blanch aerodrome. It has changed very much since we were there and is now a very busy well organised airport. We go into Algiers by car and have a drink in the Hotel Elette. We meet

Wing Commander Wisdom, the Airforce Public Relations Officer there and he says that he had heard we were coming to Algiers and that we are staying at his villa. We go up there at lunch time and find that it is a beautiful house with a large garden high up overlooking Algiers Bay. There are also about six other public relations men there, some RAF and some Army. Wing Commander Wisdom is a charming personality and he has a great sense of humour. This can be appreciated at meal times when he takes his place at the head of the table.

4th February: Thursday. I spend the morning with Cameron sunbathing on the flat roof. Write to Marie. One of the P.R. Officers, Flying Officer Matthews commonly known as Jessie, is a very interesting chap. He is the British Monotone news reporter and has a craze for dismantling bombs. It is apparently quite a common thing to go down on a morning and find him taking an unexploded bomb to pieces that he has dug out of the ground somewhere. I go into Algiers in the afternoon and have dinner at the Fin Gourmet Restaurant in the evening. Then I return to the villa at 8.0 o'clock and meet Air Marshall Sir William Welch - the Air Officer commanding Eastern Air Command.

5th February: Friday. Cameron and I go to see a French film at the Elette cinema in the afternoon. I meet up with Phil Kendall for dinner at the Fin Gourmet at night.

6 February: Saturday. Sunbathe all morning and write to Marie. Go to see a Circus in the afternoon with Cameron and Ronnie Steed. He is a reporter for the New York Herald and the Times and is an excellent type. I have dinner at the villa at night and meet the new Air Commodore.

7 February: Sunday. At 7.30 am we have a game of soccer. Public Relations Officers versus Visitors with wine. Wing Commander Wisdom is the Referee. Then sunbathe all morning again. I go to Eastern Air Command with Squadron Leader Guthrie in the afternoon. Have a shower there and dinner at the villa. Get a letter from Marie.

8 February: Monday. Sunbathe and write all morning. In the afternoon we go to see an English Film, "Raffles." Not very good. We drink at the villa at night. A new Public Relations Officer arrives from Castel Beneto, Tripoli. He has flown over the desert this morning.

9 February: Tuesday. We play another soccer game at 7.30 am and lose. Sunbathe. Then we go to see the cabaret at the Casino in the afternoon over champagne. There is a party at the villa at night. The Wing Commander asks me to entertain a torpedoed nurse. Not very nice. Hope Marie does not mind.

10 February: Wednesday. Go to a Cinema show at the American Red Cross building in the afternoon. No good. Go into the Casino to drink champagne. We have dinner at Le Tavern with Ronnie Steed, Val Phillips and John Lewis. Johnnie Player broadcasts to America at night and is very good.

11 February: Thursday. Cameron and I have a walk into Algiers in the morning and go to the Elette. This time have dinner at the Hotel L'Oasis.

12 February: Friday. Sunbathe. Go to Casino with Cameron, Bill Draper and Hugo (Spitfire boys) in the afternoon. Return to the villa again for dinner and drinks. The Wing Commander is out for the evening.

13 February: Saturday. Wing Commander Wisdom lends us his Humber Snipe and, after picking up Charlie and Phil Kendall, we get back to Setif at 4.0 o'clock in the afternoon. After dinner we go to bed early.

14 February: Sunday. I write all morning. Charlie has tummy trouble so we are not on the programme at night.

15 February: Monday. Windy day. I am operations officer and supervise the laying of the Flare Path. Spend the night in the Operations room which is in a glass building on a tower. It is very cold.

16 February: Tuesday. Group Captain Atcherley comes round to the mess at night. He says the war with Germany will definitely be over this year. I have an upset stomach so I go to bed early.

17 February: Wednesday. I am feeling much better today. We are on the programme again tonight. We do a night flying test in the afternoon and take a look at the surrounding country. It chiefly consists of high snow-capped mountains. When dusk falls the weather is poor so I sleep at dispersal. The news from the 1st Army is not good. The Americans have retreated forty miles and the Hun has captured three airfields.

18 February: Thursday. Very windy day. Little news. Americans retreat another 15 miles. Strong gale again at night and snow fall. Cameron and I sleep in fear and trembling of losing our tent.

19 February: Friday. Very misty day. I should go to Tingley to do readiness at night so I go up to the aerodrome with the C.O. and ring the Meteorological Officer at Bone. The fog is apparently going to get worse and the clouds are down over the surrounding mountains so we decide to scrub The Tingley readiness and stand by here. Go back to the mess and play Monopoly with some of the types.

20 February: Saturday. It rains all day and there is still mist and fog about. The mail comes and I get six letters from Marie and three from Scarborough. It is a great thrill and I spend all afternoon reading and answering them. The Coldstream Guards have counter attacked in Central Tunisia and are holding the front.

21 February: Sunday. Little or no news. There is minimal enemy activity lately so we spend most of our time reading and writing.

22 February: Monday. The Americans retreat a further ten miles. Stronger forces are supposed to be arriving so they should be able to check this local advance soon.

23 February: Tuesday. Do some formation flying in the afternoon with Cameron Cox and take an Adjutant up with me. We fly over the 8000 foot mountains to Boujie. The scenery on the snowcapped mountains is magnificent.

24 February: Wednesday. On the programme again. Do a night flying test in the afternoon and fly over to Maison Blanche. Very thick clouds over the Mountains on the way back and have some difficulty in getting through it. The weather closes at night.

25 February: Thursday. Very little news. The British are holding the Huns in central Tunisia now. We have recently got a lot more new crews on the Squadron and the mess is full of strange faces. We now total twenty eight crew and fifteen aeroplanes. A very unsatisfactory situation from our point of view.

26 February: Friday.   Have to carry out a test of new equipment near Biserta at night so I test the aeroplane in the afternoon.   It rains and hails and gets worse at night so I am unable to do it.

27 February: Saturday.   The British are pushing the Huns back in Central Tunisia.   Understand the Americans had heavy losses when they lost ground last week. I test an aircraft again in the afternoon and take off at 9.0 o'clock at night to do the test near Biserta. Have to fly at 15,000 feet to get above thunderstorms along the coast. Talk to poor old Squadron Leader Brown on the air. He seems to be in rather a tight fix but is determined to stay there. He is our Ground Control Interception Operator and has been landed at Cape Serratt with his mobile G.C.I. behind enemy lines to enable him to pick up German aircraft flying troops across the Sicilian Straits. This proves very successful particularly for day fighters. We land after two and a half hours.

28 February: Sunday.   British and Americans are still holding the central front and have advanced slightly.

1 March: Monday.   It is a very hot day.   I fly Johnnie Player and Peter Dunning White over to Maison Blanche in the morning. It is very pleasant flying past the 8000 foot snowcapped mountains. We take off from Maison Blanche and fly over to the advanced bomber station at St Robert. The country scenery is a good contrast. It is chiefly flat brown desert with a few dried up lakes here and there. I came here to try and get our cinematograph back to give the boys a show but it is being repaired so have to leave it. Fly back to Setif in the afternoon.

2 March: Tuesday. We are on readiness at Tingley at night. Fly over there with Flying Officer Moss, one of the new pilots, in the afternoon. A large sweep of bombers and Spitfires are going out to do a job as we land. They all return safely an hour and a half later. We are not called out during the night but it is very cold and there is nowhere that we can sleep so we are very pleased to take off again at six in the morning for Setif.

3 March: Wednesday. We have recently got some new MK V11 Beaufighters fitted with a new type of Aerial Interception set. It is a very different technique so Charlie and I take one up in the afternoon to practise with it. We get quite good results but it will require much more practice. Go into Setif town for a drink in the evening with the Commanding Officer, Val Phillips and the Adjutant. Come back to the mess for dinner.

4 March: Thursday. Go into Setif again in the afternoon for a haircut and a Turkish bath. There is some talk about the Squadron having to do a daylight operation in the Sicilian straits. It sounds rather a suicide job and we are all rather hoping it does not come off.

5 March: Friday. I start with a bad cold and go to bed early at night. Hear that Cape Serratt has been captured but Squadron Leader Brown got out alright.

6 March: Saturday. My cold is worse and I stay in bed all morning. Daylight job still sounds as though it will come off.

7 March: Sunday. My cold is still bad. I am Duty Operations Officer at night and have to spend the night in the

Control Room. My nose starts to bleed at 5.0 o'clock in the morning and it takes two hours to stop it.

8 March: Monday. More nose bleeding, in fact it bleeds most of the morning. I always seem to have this trouble after a cold. Have some excellent news in the afternoon that Johnnie Player has been promoted to a Wing Commander and taken over command of the Squadron. Everybody is very pleased about this because Johnnie is quite the most popular C.O. it would be possible to have. The 8th Army have had another victory. Apparently Rommel fell into a carefully laid trap and is now in full retreat.

9 March: Tuesday. Johnnie Player comes back from Algiers in the afternoon and we throw a small party in the Mess at night for the departure of Wing Commander Kelly and the arrival of Wing Commander Player.

10 March: Wednesday. Cameron Cox, Jeff Humes and Steve and myself set off to Boujie in the three tonner. There is some excellent scenery on the way between the high mountains. We all go to the cinema in Boujie in the afternoon.

11 March: Thursday. We are staying in small holiday bungalows on the sands. Charlie Hill goes swimming and gets washed out with a current onto a rock. We go out to get him off in a little surf boat with a rope from the beach.

12 March and 13 March: No news of interest.

14 March: Sunday. Return to Setif. See Johnnie about my rest.

15 March: Monday. I understand the Squadron is to start intruding over Sardinia in a few days. Do some more practice with MK V11.

16 March: Tuesday. Nothing of interest.

17 March: Wednesday. Group Captain Atcherley rings me up in the mess telling me that Charlie and I have been awarded D.F.C.'s. A very hectic party starts and Charlie and all the sergeants come over to the mess. Get rather drunk.

18 March: Thursday. Understand intruding starts tomorrow.

19 March: Friday. Peter Dunning White is made "B" Flight Commander and promoted to a Squadron Leader. He puts all the "B" Flight crews' names in a hat and takes three out for intruding tonight over Sardinia. I am one of them. The programme is cancelled owing to insufficient data in the afternoon, so I go to do readiness at Tingley at night. I take off at 4.30 am to patrol over a large convoy. No activity.

20 March: Saturday. Sunbathe all morning. It is a very hot day. Get an airgraph from Marie. The intruding is cancelled at night.

21 March: Sunday. Six crews go over to Bone aerodrome in the afternoon for intruding. Our headquarters is an old house which has many bomb scars on it. I am third on the programme and stand by with two other crews all night but as there is no activity in Sardinia we do not fly.

22 March: Monday. I fly Group Captain Atcherley back to Setif. Sunbathe all afternoon and write.

23 March: Tuesday. Went over to Bone again in the afternoon. The old bombed house is better organised and we now have cooking facilities for the cooks. I take off for an intruder patrol at 8.0 o'clock but have to return to Bone owing to engine trouble. The runway is very short for night landings. Mike Gloster takes off later and flies over Sardinia. He flies at an aircraft in the Circuit of a Hun aerodrome and claims a 'damage'.

24 March: Wednesday. Return to Setif. Bring two Intelligence officers with me. The A.O.C. comes in the morning and we have a discussion on intruding. I go and have a sulphur bath in the afternoon with Peter in some natural spring baths. They are very good.

25 March: Thursday. I write all morning. One of the "A" flight people went over Sardinia last night but there was no activity.

26 March: Friday. Go for a Turkish bath in Setif in the afternoon with Doc Brennan and Jeff Humes. In the evening we go to a concert given by members of the Wing.

27 March: Saturday. During the morning I do an endurance test in one of the new Beaus. Play Soft Ball in the afternoon against the sergeants.

28 March: Sunday. A very wet day. Play Soft Ball against the Airmen in the evening.

29 March: Monday. Still raining. "A" Flight unable to get back from Bone so they do readiness again.

The 8th Army takes Gabes and the Americans are pushing forward.

30 March: Tuesday. I go over to Bone in the afternoon. I am 4th on the intruder programme but it is a bad evening and we do not fly.

31 March: Wednesday. We are doing readiness again tonight so we stay at Bone. Go into the town. It has been badly knocked about with the bombing and there are few buildings that do not have battle scars. We go to a cinema. Do an air test in the afternoon. Before I take off an American Mitchell lands from a raid in Bizerta. The rear gunner has been badly wounded in the chest and we run and get an ambulance for him. He looks very white and has lost a lot of blood but the Doctor says he will live. The weather continues to rain and again we do no flying.

1 April: Thursday. Take off for Setif at 8.0 o'clock. The weather is terrible. Climb up through the rain but find a slight improvement at Setif. Go for a Sulphur bath with Peter and Phil etc. in the afternoon.

2 April: Friday. Go over to Bone again in the afternoon. The weather is still very bad and their homing apparatus unserviceable. I have to fly well out to sea to break cloud. The weather continues to deteriorate all night so we do not fly.

3 April: Saturday. Quite an improvement in the weather. Fly back to Setif at 8.0 o'clock. At night Jeff Humes goes intruding over Sardinia and does not return. Have no idea what happened to him. Think he must have been shot down by flack.

4th April: Sunday.   I go over to Bone in the afternoon. It is a beautiful day so we go down to the sea for a swim before readiness time. At 8.30 pm I set course for intruding over Sardinia. It is reported that several torpedo bombers have taken off to attack a Convoy approaching Bone and it is my job to go back and try to destroy them over their own aerodromes. A Beaufighter from 600 Squadron attacks a JU 88 about 40 miles out to sea. It is quite close to us and we see it go down. It takes nearly an hour to fly to Sardinia and it is a very dark night. We are rather annoyed because our air interception set becomes unserviceable when we are ten miles from the enemy coast and we are therefore not able to detect any night fighters which may come up behind us.   As we approach the coast, I change height frequently and fly a very erratic course in case we are being followed.   Presently I see the dark slope of the Sardinian coastline coming up before me.   It is quite easy to pinpoint my exact position by the Island of St Pietro. It is apparently a good thing to fly fast over enemy territory so I increase to 260 miles per hour .

From the Island, I set course for the aerodrome of Deccem which I have been told is where the Huns come from but, when I get there, I find that all the lights are out and there is no sign of any aircraft trying to land. From here we fly on to the other two aerodromes, Elmas and Villicedno, but again there is no sign of activity. At Elmas we find a powerful flashing beacon which enables us to pinpoint ourselves exactly. For three quarters of an hour we fly round these aerodromes in the hope that one of them will light up for an aircraft to land but nothing happens. The blackout in Sardinia is poor and it is quite easy to see towns as we go over them. At 10.15 pm we leave the island and set course for our 270 mile run back to Setif where we land at 11.45 pm.

5 April: Monday. Nothing of interest today. We have a film show on the Camp at night, "Mrs Minniver." It is very good.

6 April: Tuesday. Fly to Bone in the afternoon. It is very hot there so we go down to the beach for a swim which is enjoyable and we find the remains of a Savoi Machetti on the shore. I think it must have been one that Johnnie Player shot down in December. Phil Kendall sets off on an intruder patrol at 8.30 pm and I take off for Sardinia at 11.30 pm. The weather is not very good over there and, as it is a pitch black night, I have some difficulty recognising the coast. I fly inland and pick up the flashing beacon at Elmas. I cannot understand why the Hun leaves the Beacon on all the time because it is a very useful navigational aid for us. For the next hour we patrol over the three aerodromes of Elmas, Deccimunde and Villicedro but no aircraft take off or come into land. At 1.30 pm we set course for Setif again and land there at 3.0 o'clock.

7 April: Wednesday. We have moved the Camp nearer the aerodrome because the Doc says it will be a healthier area in the hot weather. The only snag is that we have to sacrifice the little cottage that we are using as a mess and use a large marquee instead.

8 April 9 April: No news of interest. The 8th Army are making staggering headway and are past the important Port of Sfax.

10 April: Saturday. I am the aerodrome Control Officer. Frankie Street went intruding last night and threw some beer bottles out over the Hun aerodrome. Shortly afterwards he saw a fire start on the aerodrome though I doubt if it had anything to do with his bottles.

11 April: Sunday.   The weather is now getting very hot, often over 100 degrees.   It is stifling in our tent and the mess marquee is almost unbearable for meals so we try to find shade from trees which are few and far between.   Flight Mechanics, Radar and Radio people often have to work inside the Beau's on the ground and the heat inside the aircraft is intense.   On top of this they are at great risk from the frequent strafing and bombing by enemy planes.   Even for aircrew it is quite an ordeal taxiing round and waiting to take off for night flying tests.

12 April: Monday.   We are on the night programme and fly over to Bone in the afternoon.   Doc Brennan is there and he runs us to the beach for a swim before readiness.   Two people take off on intruder patrols at 8.0 o'clock and at 9.0 o'clock there is an air raid on Bone.   The gun barrage has improved a lot and I don't think they did much damage.   At 1.30 am I am ordered off to chase two aircraft approaching Bone at 20,000 feet.   We climb up as quickly as possible but the Huns turn back before reaching Bone.   This left us with a long stern chase and, although we were flying at maximum speed for 100 miles, we were still 12 miles behind so the pursuit was abandoned.   The temperature at 20,000 feet is minus 18 degrees so we were pleased to lose height.   We continued the patrol but there was no further activity before we returned to base at 3.30 am.

13th April: Tuesday.   This day proves to be the most exciting flying operation that we have yet had to do.   For some time now we have all been aware that when the night raids tapered off we would be called upon to do daylight operations.   This has always been viewed as a pretty dangerous prospect because, whilst the Beaufighter is a very good nightfighter, it is not as fast or manoeuverable as the German Messerschmitt and Focke Wulf single seater day fighters that we are likely to encounter. Any sort of conflict with them could prove pretty fatal for us.

The story started at lunchtime when Johnnie Player received an order from Group for Beau's to patrol the Sardinian Coast in the afternoon in the hope of intercepting some torpedo bombers. These were expected to attack a convoy, which was sailing down the Mediterranean destined for Algiers, at dusk. This was the largest convoy ever to sail to North Africa. The Navy asked us to do everything possible to stave off the Torpedo Bombers which are a greater risk to them than German submarines. The Bombers are wise enough not to fly through our Radar controlled areas and would certainly keep at sea level to avoid Radar detection. Our only chance of intercepting them is therefore to put up standing patrols at sea level along the Sardinian west coast as it is known that they will take off form airfields in Sardinia. This means that we will be patrolling within German fighter range. It is approximately 200 miles to the chosen area and Johnnie Player has decided that sections of three shall patrol the coast, relieving one another until dusk.

The first section known as Red will be led by Johnnie with Hugh Elliot as his number two and and Cameron Cox as number three taking off at 3.0 o'clock. The second section, Green section, will be led by Mike Gloucester with Gordon Sprawl and a new pilot, Humphries, as two and three. I am to lead the third Blue section with Frankie Street as my number two and Kevin O'Sullivan as my number three. At 4.45 we took off and set course for the patrol line. I checked our position as we crossed the coast and set the stop watch. As it is a 200 mile sea trip at low level to our position, our navigation has to be accurate to be sure that we patrol in the right place. We flew in a fairly wide formation as low as possible to avoid Radar detection and an hour later arrived to commence the first leg of our patrol. After a few minutes we saw a flight of aircraft at the south end of the line but this was a false alarm as it turned out to be Green section finishing their shift. This was rather alarming because at first we took them to be torpedo bombers. Charlie is peering into the sky looking for hostile fighters although if he saw one I don't know what on earth we should do about it.

After five minutes I hear Frankie yell, "Look Dougie, over on our starboard." A quick glance was enough to see the large formation of aircraft flying as low as ourselves. It is the first time I have had the job of attacking enemy planes in the day time and the sight of all those black shapes makes my heart pound so heavily that I can almost feel it pushing my tunic in and out. I swing our section over to starboard and get into position astern of the formation. From here I estimate that there are 12 to 18 of them and that they are all torpedo bombers. They have spotted us now and I can see the exhaust smoke coming from them all as they open their throttles to full speed. We ease up slowly behind them in line abreast and, as I get closer, I can see the colossal amount of machine gun fire. They all seem to have two guns in their rear turrets so there are about 36 firing at us and I can see the sea in front of our section splashing furiously as the bullets strike. It looks impossible to fly into it without being shot down.

I call up Frankie and Kevin, the two others in my section, and say that we will try and split up the formation before concentrating on any one plane. Our cannons have a slightly longer range than their guns so for a minute we stay just out of range and fire our shells into the group. Whilst we cannot be sure of accurate results at this range it is obviously very disturbing for the Huns.

They still seem to be holding their formation so we decide to pull to echelon starboard and try a quarter attack. I dive in first and get a good burst in at the back of the Hun and Frankie and Kevin follow and do the same. Then we pull round and come back into line abreast again. At last this does the trick. The Huns, obviously unnerved, climb up and drop their valuable torpedoes into the sea. I count about twenty plunging into the water and several others later. There is some very inadequate cloud about a thousand feet above and they split up like a lot of frightened hens to take cover. One of them turns and flies over me to drop his torpedo, obviously trying to hit my aircraft. It is very wide and I turn hard to follow two JU 88's that are making for the cloud. I pull up into range behind one of them just as he is coming out of the top and fire a long burst into him. I see a lot of black smoke pouring from his port engine and then he slips back behind the cloud. I am very tempted to dive through it to see if he hits the sea but I glimpse the other JU 88 ahead and decide to have a crack at him. This man is obviously more experienced because he starts turning furiously, trying to get on my tail. A Beau does not turn very well but I manage to bank harder than he does and to pull to the inside of the circle. By this time I am extremely close and can see the large black crosses and swastikas on its fuselage and wings. I can also see the two guns on its back turret flashing away towards me. It is not easy to do any accurate shooting when turning like this but with some difficulty I pull my sights in front of the Hun and fire a long burst into him. By this time the Gerry gunner is just about getting our range and I hear a whistle from Charlie in the back followed by something about "bloody close." Later this proved to be a bullet through his cupola which couldn't have missed his head by more than a quarter of an inch.

At this point Frankie Street calls me and says, "I've got a fan knocked out and a bullet in the leg." Unfortunately I am too occupied with my JU 88 to reply to him at the time and so I keep my sights on the Hun and finish the rest of my ammunition off. The JU 88 is obviously hit a good many times and the rear gunner has stopped firing. I think I have killed him alright. Finally it disappeared into a cloud and as no smoke was coming from it, I could not claim more than a 'damaged'. Now I start to worry about Frankie. I call him up and get no reply. In fact I call him for the next hour all the way home but it seems obvious that he was badly hit and crashed into the sea. I also call Kevin and am relieved to hear his cheery voice telling me he is O.K. The rest of the bombers have scattered in all directions and are making for Sardinia again as quickly as they can. Kevin is not in sight so we both make our own way home again, he to Bone and me to Setif.

I am rather worried on the way back that some trouble may develop because with one bullet in the fuselage it is logical to expect several more in the wings and engines. That hour's flight back to the mainland seems to be one of the longest trips I have ever done. We cross the coast at Djellie and climb over the hills back to Setif.

We land safely and are welcomed by a crowd of excited Airmen anxious to know what had happened. Half an hour later Green section starts coming back with the good news that they had run into several of the struggling Huns making for Sardinia. Mike Gloster claimed to have destroyed a Dornier 217 and Humphries another JU 88. In the mess tonight the Intelligence officer is very busy getting everybody's story and at 9.0 o'clock he announces the score as two confirmed, one probably destroyed and three 'damaged', Kevin having accounted for two 'damaged'.

122

I feel quite sure that Frankie destroyed one before he was shot down but as, we had no proof, no claim could be made. Johnnie Player is very pleased with the show and says we achieved our main objective in making them drop their torpedoes and return to Sardinia.

14 April: Wednesday. Whilst yesterday was a most successful day for the Squadron from a victory point of view, it was also a black 13th from a loss point of view. Beaus have been searching all day for Frankie but at night all have the same tale to tell. No sign of Frankie. On top of this John Thorp who was operating out of Algiers had a chase on a low flying aircraft which dropped a depth charge into the sea. The explosion blew John up and he crashed into the water, killing both himself and his operator. Also Flying Officer Campbell crashed a Beau at Bone breaking a couple of ribs. His operator got away unscathed but the aircraft was completely destroyed by fire.

We receive a signal from the Navy in Algiers in the afternoon congratulating us on an excellent show. They say that not one torpedo bomber attacked them and that the whole convoy arrived at Algiers without loss. We also have a message from the Commodore thanking us for an excellent effort. In the afternoon Johnnie Player calls me into his office and informs me that I have been posted back to England for a rest with effect from the16th April.

15 April: Thursday. Spend most of the day packing. In the afternoon the airmen ask me to go and have some champagne with them before I leave. They say some very complimentary things about Charlie and I and I return to my packing slightly the worse for wear. We have a Beaufighter out all day again looking for Frankie but still no sign of him so we can only assume that he was killed when he crashed.

There is a very slim possibility that the Huns may have picked him up because they would obviously search the scene of the battle for their own men. Peter has a large birthday party at the hotel at Hamman at night and about thirty of us go there for dinner. Johnnie makes a toast to me and I have to respond with a couple of speeches. Have rather too much to drink at the end of the evening.

16 April: Friday. Pack the rest of my gear and fly over to Algiers with Flying Officer Moss. Then I go to the Air Reinforcement Pool to await arrangements for my passage home. It looks as if it will be better to go by sea because there is a large waiting list to travel by air. I don't really like the sea, particularly these U boat infected waters but as I have now not got an aeroplane or a Squadron, I shall take the first opportunity that comes. Charlie and I share a room in a modern block of flats.

17 April: Saturday. Meet Peter Dunning White and Cameron Cox outside the Elete Hotel as arranged. We go to a cinema in the afternoon and have dinner at the Hotel L'Oasis at night. There is rather a heavy raid on Algiers while we are eating and fifteen people including some nuns are killed two buildings away from the L'Oasis. The French people in the hotel are remarkably calm and most of them continue dining but I cannot help thinking that it is only due to the presence of English officers that they try to be so brave. The French have a strong respect for the way Londoners put up with heavy raids and I can tell by the sheepish looks we keep getting that they are trying to equal them.

In the afternoon we meet an admiral who is a friend of Cameron's father and we have some drinks with him. He was in command of the big convoy and was very grateful to us for our daylight attack on the bombers.

18 April: Sunday. Meet Peter again at the Elete Hotel. We go to Le |Paris for lunch and to the Tavern Hotel for dinner at night. There is another air raid on Algiers but the Tavern is not quite as near the docks as the Oasis so it is less disturbing. Say farewell to Peter. He is going back to Setif tomorrow.

19 April: Monday. There is nothing of interest to write. Most of my time is spent sorting my kit and going for walks. Johnnie Wright, Charlie Hill, Steve and Arthur Woolley arrive. They are also going home for a rest.

24 April: Saturday. Our boat sails today. We are all up at 7.0 o'clock and down at the docks at 9.30. Charlie Hill has rather a scare when the embarkation officer arrives and says that his passage has been cancelled. Fortunately an hour later this proves to be a mistake and he joins us again. Our ship is a converted luxury liner and is extremely comfortable. There are very few people going back on it and practically all are either Air force or Army officers. We have an excellent cabin which I share with Johnnie Wright and Steve. The food is also absolutely first class and is an enormous change from the diet we have been used to. We sail in the late afternoon. The sea is very calm and the boat practically motionless. At night we have a few drinks in the bar and go to bed early.

25 April: Easter Saturday. We have a muster parade on the deck every morning and it is arranged that we shall have a roster for manning the ship's anti-aircraft guns. At night we are in the cinema when we approach the Straits. There is a slight disturbance in the middle of the film when we hear several explosions. The ship shudders but it proves to be one of our escorts dropping a depth charge. There are apparently usually a few U boats in this vicinity.

26 April: Monday. We have passed through the Straits and the sea is now not quite so calm. I do a two hour watch on one of the Ack Ack guns in the afternoon and in the evening we have another film.

27 April: Tuesday. Johnnie, Steve, Charlie Hill and I are all on the guns from 8.0 o'clock in the morning until 12.30 pm. The sea is very rough and there is a high gale blowing. We are all pleased when our four and a half hour watches are finished.

20 April: Wednesday. The sea is still very rough and the ship is pitching badly but I am pleased that I have no feeling of sea sickness. At night there is another film on the ship and we go to bed early because we have to be on our guns from 4.0 am until 8.0 am in the morning.

29 April: Thursday. The early morning shift is very unpleasant and cold and we are pleased to get down to a hot breakfast. The sea continues rough and we sleep for the rest of the morning. We are on the guns from 8.0 until 12.0 again tonight and are just going up to our watch when the ships siren goes. I get my gun loaded and ready and have a look round through the binoculars at two low flying aircraft which I can just see a long way off circling the convoy. They are powerful binoculars and it is quite obvious to me that they are two Focke Wulf Condors. Their large broad tails give them away. They have evidently sighted us and are circling to find the best way to attack us.

The sun is setting low and my guess that they would try and take advantage of this proves correct. After about ten minutes, Steve shouts from his gun that he can see one of them coming from the west. I pick it up. It is flying at about 5,000 feet towards the middle of the convoy. Ours is the largest ship and in the centre so I expect we are a likely target for him.

Condor makes a steady run towards us and when he is roughly in range, I open fire with my 20 millimetre cannon. Steve, Charlie Hill and Johnnie are also firing several other guns at the front of the ship. It is difficult to keep a steady sight when the ship is swaying about but my rounds appear to be pretty near him. He drops one bomb which lands between our ship and the next one doing no damage apart from sending a large column of water up into the air. The Condor passes straight over our ship and I fire at the large four engined shape until it is out or range again. Whilst he is circling round to do another run, I am very busy putting a new drum of ammunition on my gun. I find a stoppage in the breech from the last rounds and have some difficulty in removing it. Another ten minutes and he is spotted coming in again from the west and again we fire at him whilst he is in range. This time his bomb landed well behind our ship, safely missing the others.

I think our fire is probably upsetting his aim quite a lot but I don't think we have done much damage to him so far. When I think of the four guns I have in my Beau and the short range that we are used to, it is difficult to imagine doing much damage with one of them at this range. However, I should imagine the psychological effect of the tracer shells coming up at the crew must be hard to ignore. The Hun is now turning round for a third attack and I change another pan of ammunition. This attempt is very similar to the other two except that the column of water from his bomb seems to be wider than ever. It must have been his last one because he does not come in again. We are all expecting him to return and do a low sweep at dusk but there is no sign of him. The Captain's main worry now is whether he will have given our position away to the U boats because these Condors in the Atlantic usually do the spotting for them. Anyway this is apparently not the case because the rest of the night is quite uneventful.

30 April: Friday. The ship has started rolling rather badly again now and I have some difficulty sleeping in my bunk. We do a two hour watch in the afternoon and see the film Lady Hamilton at night.

1st May: Saturday. We play cards all morning and do a two hour watch again in the afternoon. At 4.0 o'clock we see the coast of Northern Ireland on our starboard side.

The convoy is continuing up the west coast. The approaches to the English Channel are still at great risk from Focke-Wulf Condors and submarines and we have therefore to go round Ireland and down to Liverpool.

2 and 3 May: are uneventful.

4th May: We disembark at Liverpool.

I am now without a Squadron and have been instructed to contact A.M. Postings on my arrival in England. They have informed me that I can take 14 days leave and will be told of my posting in a few days time. I gathered that it was likely to be either Instructing or a Radar experimental unit and said that I would prefer the latter. I had told Marie in a letter that I expected to arrive home at about the beginning of May and she had gone back to the Stamford Bridge near Chester with Yvette and Suzanne. It was quite a short journey from Liverpool and it was wonderful to see them all again looking so well and happy.

The following day we all travelled back to Horsforth for two weeks and I was able to forget all about the war, even finding time to paint our house. I received a letter, however, informing me that I should report to T.F.U. Defford Defensive section at the end of my leave. This is about eight miles from Worcester and I had to be there on 18th May. Our Hillman car had been left in the garage while I was abroad, so I was able to use it to travel down.

Defford is in the vicinity of Malvern College in the Malvern Hills where scientists had developed the airborne Radar which we used in North Africa. Because this had a range only equal to the height of the aircraft, they were producing, amongst other things, a disc scanner to fit in the nose giving a much longer range that could be used down to sea level. These scientists, university products whom we call boffins, invariably smoked pipes and wore old tweed suits. They made frequent use of our Mess and we were encouraged to get to know them.

Most days were fairly routine. I would report to Flights each morning and Squadron Leader Cook, the Flight Commander, would detail two or three flights for the day with either Radar Mechanics or boffins to test out experimental Radar equipment. Quite often there would be a bang and a flash and a string of swear words from which we concluded that the set had blown and we must return to base.

129

The most interesting thing about Defford was that they had almost all the different aircraft in the RAF and I was called on to fly Spitfires, Hurricanes, American Bostons, Wellingtons, Swordfish and the new Mosquitos. Because we were not concerned with operations, they were generous with 48 hour passes and I was able to get home to Marie more often. As the rest period was going to be of short duration, we decided not to leave the house and live out until my next tour of operations.

Early September was the anniversary of "Battle of Britain" week during which period Councils up and down the country organised events to raise money to buy Spitfires. A dance was held in the Officers mess and Marie was able to come down to attend it. The enemy had just been driven out of Africa and the invasion of Sicily was just about to begin. The news reels at the cinemas were very full of these events. Because I had just returned from this theatre with stories to tell and a D.F.C., the Council of Worcester asked me if I could give talks in the intervals to boost funds. During the evening, the Mayor of Worcester invited Marie to stay for a few days and we were able to spend time together. A friend of mine, Jack Etchells, had arrived at Defford after completing a tour with Bomber command and on days off we took full advantage of our free membership of Worcester golf club. The members here were very friendly and we played several times a week.

Marie's mother was understandably concerned about her living alone in a strange town with the babies and, as she had a young housemaid, she arranged for her to go to Horsforth to help look after the children. This was a great relief to me as I did not like leaving her on her own. The only snag was that Edna was a very pretty young girl and it did not take long for the boys to notice. Consequently, she became a worry on her nights off when she came home very late.

I have done quite a lot of flying on Mosquitos, particularly the new Mk XX11's which have more powerful Merlin engines giving a top speed of 420 miles per hour. They are also fitted with Air Interception scanners in the nose to avoid the height limitation on range. I thought that these were by far the best aircraft and would like to fly them on my next tour of operations. Another friend of mine, Joe Singleton, was coming to the end of his rest period and was joining 25 Squadron which was being reformed and re- with these Mosquitos at Acklington. He said he would mention my name to the C.O. to see if I could join them when my rest period was over.

October and November: were uneventful months but early in **December** I was notified that I was posted to 25 Squadron with effect from 1st January 1944.

23 December: I was able to take four days leave to spend Christmas at home with Marie and the girls. As always it all went far too quickly.

28 December: I drove back to Defford for a few more exercises and then travelled north to RAF Acklington.

131

25 SQUADRON

SECOND TOUR OF OPERATIONS

I have not recently mentioned Charlie Robbins who I last saw when we left the boat at Liverpool. He had been posted to an instructing job for Radar operators at a training school. When I heard that I was going to 25 Squadron, I rang him and asked if he would like to join me for a second tour as we had done well together on the first and he said he would be very happy to do that.

It was good to meet up with Charlie again. He now has a commission so we met in the Officer's mess. Our C.O. was Wing Commander Wight Boycott and we were in "A" Flight. There were two Mosquito Mk 1V's with Mk1V Radar to get used to but Mosquito Mk XV11.s were arriving every day. These had Mk X Radar sets with scanners in the nose which slightly altered the shape giving a blunt look in place of the graceful curve of the original Mosquito. Until the end of January we were occupied with Northstead Ground Control Interception station doing practice night interceptions with the Mk X Radar which is quite a new technique to Charlie. We also have to do air to sea firing tests with the new machines.

28 January: We are fully operational and up to strength and have been informed that the Squadron is to move to R.A.F. Coltishall. It is not new to me as I had been there with 255 Squadron before we went abroad. The only fault was the rather small grass airfield when we have been

132

used to long hard runways at Defford and Acklington. This caused an unpleasant moment when I first landed a Mosquito at Coltishall. Before my arrival at Defford I had always done three point landings which entailed gliding in with engines throttled back until flying speed was lost, then a quick pull back on the stick to cause a stall when the plane would drop the last inch or two onto the ground. At Defford we were called on to fly American Boston 111's which were light bombers with tricycle undercarriages with a wheel at the front. When I asked about landing these, I was told to just roll them onto the runway, throttle back and apply the brakes. I was told the same thing when first flying Mosquitos which seemed to work quite well on the runways.

The Mosquito is a light aeroplane being made of wood and when I first landed at Coltishall my tanks were low after a long flight and I rolled it onto the grass. Unfortunately, it was far from level and when the plane hit a hump, it took to the air again and the field was too small to have a second try. I opened the engines and went round in a circle, warning Charlie to hold tight as I was intending to do a three pointer. This worked perfectly and I never again did a roller.

February: was a fairly uneventful month. As we appear to be stationed here for some time, I enquired about living out. The adjutant said this was allowed so I looked round for a suitable place. The Norfolk Broads was a popular holiday area for boating people before the war and I discovered that a river joined the Broads at Wroxam near the aerodrome. There were quite a number of holiday bungalows on the river side which seemed to be empty. I found the owner of one of these who was agreeable to renting it and took a 48 hour leave to tell Marie about it.

We had a bad experience letting our own house to a writer two years ago who left it such a terrible state that Marie had to evict her so she is understandably reluctant to repeat the experience. However, a family called Pettys, printers in Leeds, whose daughter was getting married, persuaded her to rent it to them.

The bungalow was right on the edge of the river and I had to put wire netting round it so that the children would not fall in. When it was ready Marie, Yvette and Suzanne came down with Edna and we had a very pleasant time there.

Hitler seems to have given up the idea of invading England and is now fully engaged with Russia. For this reason, there are less big raids and the enemy aircraft are mostly fighter bombers intruding or bombing factories. When they do come it is usually in bad weather and flying low to try and avoid our night fighters. This is a difficult period doing long low level patrols at night in very bad weather and we lose two crews in February and March.

At this time, I had rather an unfortunate occurrence which put me out of favour with the C.O. This was just before Marie came down when, on a 48 hour pass, I had arranged to borrow the squadron Magister to fly up to see her. The Magister is a small two seater aircraft and when on the ground the engine cowling rather obscures the view whilst taxiing. It was a wet period and there were cones in places where the grass was soft. Unfortunately, I missed one of these and as it passed under the wing, it punched a small hole in the wood. It was obviously not safe to take off so I took it to the Hanger to be repaired. However, the C.O. had booked it for the following day and was annoyed that the incident had upset his arrangements. I was duly summoned to his office and given a severe reprimand. Although I took this without comment, I felt it very unjustified as I had not previously damaged any aircraft through neglect.

The accident would have been quickly forgotten but for the fact that the C.O. landed a Mosquito a few days later at night and taxied into a petrol tanker. This started a fire and caused considerable damage to both the Mosquito and the tanker. From then on he avoided me in the mess and for the rest of the time he was on the Squadron. At the end of April, he moved to another Station and Willum Hoy was promoted to Wing Commander and appointed C.O. with whom I had excellent relations.

From North Africa, the American and British Armies had occupied Sicily and were preparing to invade Italy. In Russia the tables had been turned and the Russians were advancing on all fronts. RAF Bomber Command were mounting 1000 Bomber raids several times a week on the Ruhr, Hamburg and German manufacturing centres mainly from aerodromes on the East coast. The American Flying Fortresses too carried out daylight raids with hundreds of Bombers from bases in Norfolk and Lincolnshire. As a result of this, the air was getting very congested and at night our Ground Control Interception Stations had to contend with many stragglers coming through the sector. If they were sure of an enemy they would call it a Bandit and, if in doubt, it was a Bogey.

I always had a fear of shooting down a friendly aircraft and on 14th March we had been put onto a Bogey flying towards Hull. It was changing course rapidly and going up and down as if it were trying to throw night fighters off the scent. Finally Charlie got a contact at three miles. It was going faster than the usual JU 88s but at top speed we managed to gain on it and eventually got a visual on the exhaust pipe flames. I closed in until I could see the black shape but it did not seem right. A JU 88 has two rudders but this had one large fin in the middle. It was not one of our bombers which would have had four engines at this time and it was too big for a Mosquito. It was a half moon night so I pulled to the east side of the enemy which was slightly lit by the low moon, hoping that I would be in darkness. As I got close, I saw a large German cross on the fuselage and at that moment the multi-gun turret in the back opened fire on us. Fortunately, the gunner must have called out and the pilot turned the plane over and went into a steep power dive causing the fire to go over the top of us. I put our plane into a steep power dive at full throttle but he was an experienced man and dived into a large cumulus cloud. Charlie tried to pick him up again but he was too evasive.

We returned to base and I immediately went through the latest enemy aircraft identification and there was a new report on a JU 188 which was just coming into service. It had a single fin and more powerful engines. I wish I had found time to read this report earlier. The only good thing that came out of this was that a few pairs of night Binoculars started to appear on the Squadron. In my report I suggested that, if we had had a pair, I might have identified the aircraft earlier. I think probably because of this all Mosquitos were fitted with them within a week.

We have settled down to a daily routine of two nights on and two nights off. This entails reporting to Flights at about 2.0 pm to do night flying tests, which is flight testing the aeroplane, and then getting into pairs for Charlie to check the Radar which often seemed to develop a squint or some other fault that needed resetting. We then went to the Mess for tea and reported back before dusk. The Flight commander then gave us a state of readiness which is

136

immediate, 15 minutes, 30 minutes or an hour. If it was immediate, it meant sitting in Flights in flying gear with parachute harness on ready to rush out to our aircraft.

Ongoing games of poker were usually in progress whilst we waited for calls from operations and different states of readiness people would drop out when they were scrambled and take a hand when they returned. There was also a Bridge set which usually included Charlie. At dawn we would get a call from Ops telling us that we could stand down and I would drive back to Marie at Horning and go to bed and sleep until ten or eleven. We would have some time together and some lunch before I went back to Flights at two o'clock for the next night's flying tests.

14ᵗʰ March: We were scrambled for several Bogies which were coming in towards Hull. It seems that the Germans are determined to have a go at Hull, probably because, being on the east coast, they think it is an easier target. It soon turned out to be a bigger raid than expected and we were directed to a position fifty miles out from Cromer, where Charlie got a contact on a fast flying aircraft at 10.000 feet. With the Mosquito throttle override pulled out we managed to gain on him. This override was only to be used for five minutes in emergencies but it was over ten minutes before we gained a visual. This time I had no trouble identifying a Dornier 217 which was faster and more manoeuvrable than a Junkers 88. I was able to close in to 200 feet without being observed and fired a short burst. I saw that I had hit the port engine and the rear gunner immediately opened fire which was very wide of the mark. The aircraft quickly turned over into a dive. I followed it down but the flames were obviously taking hold and a minute or two later, I saw a flash and flames on the sea where it had gone in.

I called up our Ground Control Interception Station, code named Ailsa and told them that we had destroyed a Dornier. They said that there were more Bandits coming towards Hull and had we enough petrol and ammunition to take on another interception. I said that we had so they sent us back to the edge of the sector fifty miles east of Cromer. After about half an hour, they said they had another Bandit for us and gave us an interception course. We were lower than in the earlier chase but, thanks to the new Scanner Mk X Radar, Charlie was able to get a contact at five miles. The bandit was again weaving about and making rapid changes of height to try and shake us off but I also think the Germans are fitting rear facing Radar to warn them of approaching night fighters. After about ten minutes we closed in and I identified it as a new Heinkel 177 which were starting to appear. I was keeping low so that the rear gunner could not see me. I pulled up at about 150 feet and gave it a good burst. The enemy plane burst into flames, pieces started to fly off and splashes appeared on the windscreen. We saw it go straight down and hit the sea so I called up Ailsa and they told me to return to Base.

I found the splashes on the windscreen disturbing and told Charlie that I thought it was oil from the Bandits engine. He did not think so and suspected that it was the rear gunner's blood. After we landed he got a rigger to examine the windscreen and he later told me that he was right. I always found it upsetting to think of men being killed but satisfied myself that they were carrying 4000 lb bombs which would have been dropped on Hull.

The Squadron did well this night. My friend Joe Singleton had been put on the same raid and had shot down three enemy aircraft but unfortunately returned fire from the last one knocked out one of his engines. Somehow he managed to make a forced landing and he and his operator escaped with minor bruises. This was quite a feat as it is generally thought to be impossible to land a fast aircraft in a field at night.

The Luftwaffe operations have changed considerably over the last year. The mass bomber raids which had devastated our cities earlier in the war had apparently stopped. This was because the efficiency of our fighters and the radar on the ground and in the air had given them unacceptable losses. Also the Anti-aircraft guns had developed the proximity shell which had to be aimed right but would explode when it came into close contact with an aircraft.

Most people were aware that the American and British forces would be invading Europe sometime this year and it must have been obvious to all knowledgeable Germans that, with the Russians advancing and our forces landing in Italy, they had no chance of winning the war although there was no sign of them seeking surrender terms.

There were strong rumours from intelligence that Hitler was putting all his faith in secret weapons. These varied from rockets to flying bombs and nuclear devices and were said to be made in large impregnable underground factories manned by thousands of slave workers.

Apart from the relatively small raid on Hull most Bandits were smaller, faster machines like the Me 410's either trying to pick off returning bombers or intruding and dropping light bombs on our airfields.

27 March: We were scrambled to chase an intruder that had dropped a couple of bombs on our airfield but he was very fast and had a long lead on us so that we were unable to get a contact. When we returned to base a fog had descended on Coltishall and we were diverted to Corby Grange. This was a new aerodrome designed for aircraft in distress. The runway was wider and at least twice the usual length. Its main feature was flame burners down each side of the runway which lifted the fog and formed a kind of tunnel 50 or 60 feet above the ground. They had an excellent approach system so we had no difficulty in making a safe landing.

The Station was very crowded as a considerable number of returning bombers had made use of it and we had difficulty in finding anywhere to sleep. The following morning the fog lifted and we were able to return to Coltishall but not before midday and Marie was worried that I had not returned at the usual time.

30 March: A number of intruders came into our sector and Ailsa gave us a vector on one of them. It had been strafing a bomber base and was on its way back. We followed it for 120 miles but were unable to significantly close the distance even though we were using the throttle override and the engine temperature gauges were getting dangerously high. Anti-aircraft guns on the Dutch coast opened up on us so we gave up and returned to Base.

11 April: We had another abortive night when, after two long chases, we identified the planes as Mosquitos. A long third chase was abandoned when the enemy dived into low cloud, causing us to lose contact.

The searchlights usually worked in conjunction with anti-aircraft and had not been too successful. They therefore asked if we would co-operate with them. The idea was that they should cone the plane with three or four beams and that we should fly towards the intersection hoping to get a contact even if they had not got the aircraft illuminated.

12 April: Working with them we managed to get a contact but when we followed it up it turned out to be a Halifax.

20 April: We were scrambled twice. The first was a successful chase and we identified the Bandit as a JU 88 but when I pressed the firing buttons there was no response. For some reason we had lost the air pressure that operated them so we landed and had the fault repaired. At 4.30 am we were scrambled again and chased two intruders but could not get a contact on them.

The Squadron consisted of "A" Flight and "B" Flight, each having about nine aircraft. The Flights were at different parts of the Airfield and away from Station H.Q. The planes were parked in bomb bays which protected them from shrapnel so that they could only be destroyed by a direct hit. These were known as dispersal points and had flight offices, air crew quarters and maintenance sections for the ground crew. The flights were the responsibility of a Flight Commander with the rank of Squadron Leader.

Willum Hoy had been "A" Flight Commander and, as I mentioned earlier, he was appointed Commanding Officer of the Squadron when Wing Commander Wight Boycott was moved on. We were all wondering when the next Flight Commander would arrive and it was a great surprise to me to be informed that I was to have the position with a promotion to Squadron Leader. This of course carried extra responsibilities and when I am not flying I spend most of my time in the Flight Office dealing with maintenance matters and detailing the crews with their flying duties.

We are also coming up to a time when we will be intruding over Germany in conjunction with Bomber Command. This calls for patrolling between the German Fighter bases and the Bomber stream to try and intercept any fighters that take off. There could be no ground control so it will depend solely on Radar Operators picking up chance contacts. This will mean flying to Bomber Command briefings and deciding the best areas for our patrols.

We had all been aware of the massive build up of British and American forces on the south coast and that the invasion of Europe was imminent. Our forces had already invaded Italy and brought about the Italian surrender and Mussolini had fled to the German occupied north. It was therefore a matter of great excitement when it was announced to the world on 5th June that the landings in Normandy had been successful.

In the meantime, things were going on much the same on the Squadron with pilots continuing to co-operate whenever possible with the searchlights. The Ground Control interception stations usually had two fighters on patrol but could only handle one interception at a time and this is when we sent surplus fighters to work with the searchlights.

7 June: We had two crews on patrol with Ailsa so we took off to work with the searchlights. After a while we saw the beams concentrating and flew towards the cone. Charlie picked up a contact and after a very erratic chase I was able to identify it as a Me 410. It was doing in access of 400 miles per hour so we were stretched to catch up. I think the pilot expected the usual anti-aircraft fire when caught in the searchlights as he was not taking any evasive action when we closed in. I gave a two second burst of fire at 200 feet which caused flames to spread to the engines and it went straight down and hit the sea.

For the rest of June we kept up our night patrols over the sea but there was very little enemy activity, probably because the Luftwaffe were concentrating all their efforts on Normandy. Most of our day fighter squadrons were focused on the landings and had almost complete air supremacy in that area.

Reports were now coming through of flying bombs landing in the London area and one night when Willum Hoy had taken off to investigate a Bogey in the south, Operations put him onto one of these. He said it was flying at about 4000 feet with flames from a burner at the back travelling at something in access of 450 miles per hour. He was at about 10,000 feet when he saw it but even in a dive he could not catch up with it.

We were informed that these were being launched from mobile launching pads in the Calais area which were regularly moved so that they could not be bombed. It was anticipated that hundreds would be aimed at London, day and night, in the hope that Londoners would get no respite from them.

About this time Marie and I had decided to go to London for a night, leaving Yvette and Suzanne with Edna at the bungalow. We heard a number of flying bombs going over. They sounded like noisy motor cycle engines and were quite visible at two or three thousand feet. The Londoners were as usual going quietly about their business and only if

143

the motor stopped would they drop flat to the ground. The bombs appeared to be about 3000 to 4000 lbs and did considerable damage when they did land. Fortunately, they were not accurately targeted and although Greater London covers a very wide area, large numbers of them landed in open country. The Germans called these bombs V.1's.

Plans were put in force to counter this new threat to London but the biggest problem was that fighters were not generally fast enough to catch them. Our Mosquitos would do a little over 430 miles per hour in straight flight but if we could dive from 15000 to 4000 or 5000 feet it would be possible to get up to a little over 450 miles per hour. A new day fighter, the Typhoon, has just come into service which could just about match their speed.

In order to reach London, the V.1's have to be launched in the region of Calais or Dunkirk and no more than ten or fifteen miles inland. When they are launched, the launching tubes give off a large flash. The first line of defense was therefore that Mosquitos should patrol near the French coast looking for these flashes and the jet flames from the bomb when it took to the air. The procedure was to steer towards the flash at about 15000 feet and when the bomb passed under the nose of the aircraft to roll over and do a power dive at maximum speed, hoping to pull out within firing range behind the bomb. This action required very good judgment because the bomb was only about two feet in diameter with very small wings and was a difficult target to hit.

This chase could go to within five miles of the English coast when a concentration of anti-aircraft guns would take over, using proximity shells. After this the Tornados took up the chase to the suburbs of London when the bombs would encounter a very intense balloon barrage. These operations were extremely successful and by the end of August only one bomb in seven was getting through. The best day was 28th August when 94 bombs approached the coast and only four got through. The Ack Ack guns were the most successful destroying 65, fighters accounted for 23 and the Balloons 2.

Our first patrols off Calais were code named Anti-Diver patrols and from early July most of our nights were spent doing three hour stints as there were very few intruders in our section at this time.

9 July: We did our first patrol near Calais and I realised for the first time how difficult it was going to be to shoot these things down. It was easy to see them being launched and to spot the tell tail lights approaching the Channel but with the best of timing it was extremely difficult to pull out of a dive in firing range and their speed made it impossible to close up this distance. On the occasions when we got into range, the target was so small that unless we could actually hit the jet it had little effect. Our cannons were armed with an assortment of armour piercing, incendiary and high explosive shells but as the bombs were torpedo shaped, any strikes on the side would not detonate the shell but would just be deflected.

12, 17 and 20 July: We did patrols on these nights but were now troubled with low cloud. This weather particularly suited the Germans, who could launch their bombs in any conditions but for us it was impossible to see the jet flames from 15000 feet.

28 July: The weather had improved and we made a couple of interceptions firing at maximum range. The last one seemed to be deflected from its course so we probably clipped one of the wings but, as we did not see it go down, we could not say that it was destroyed.

29 July: Thick cloud persisted and although we flew up and down the French coast for three and a half hours and saw launching flashes, we could not see tail lights and Charlie could not get any contacts.

5 August: Conditions were so bad that we had to cut short the patrol and as base was closed down we were directed to Bradwell Bay where we spent the night. The same thing happened the next day. Low fog and mist covered the Channel and although we patrolled at 10,000 feet for three and a half hours, we could not see any bombs being launched. The fog had again spread to our base and we had to land at Manston for the night.

By this time, Marie was getting used to these unexpected stop-overs when the weather closed in as Norfolk was particularly prone to low cloud. We got the idea that a dog might be a good edition to the family and found a Welsh Corgi being advertised by some people near Nottingham. It was agreed that they would leave it in the Guard room at Defford. On a night flying test one afternoon, I dropped in to collect him and Charlie looked after him as we flew back to Coltishall.

10, 13, 14, 17 and 18 August: The weather improved and we carried out more three hour patrols on these nights but could not lay claim to any bombs destroyed. We had got in firing range several times and the targets had swerved and even dived as our shells hit the wings but they may well have recovered. On the last one, Charlie had been unable to join me and I took along a new operator. We had three interceptions rolling over at 15,000 feet and pulling into a vertical dive to maximum speed. He was rather disturbed as he had not been used to these sort of antics at night.

Because of the flying bomb problem, the British and Canadian Armies in Normandy have made a spectacular advance to Antwerp and overwhelmed the launching sites. This relieved the situation in London although, even so, the V.1. episode had injured over 18,000 and caused more than 6000 deaths.

Due to our speed limitations, the Mosquitos have not fared too well and the third stage of defence between Dover and the Balloons has done much better. The new single seater Typhoons have a speed advantage over the bombs and are able to close into a more effective range and keep on firing until they blow up. We heard of two cases however, of Typhoons being destroyed by the explosion when they fired at under 200 feet.

The V.1.'s have a maximum range of 200 to 220 miles and as our armies advanced, they moved into Holland. We continued our patrols off the coast but there were now very few and most dropped well short of London. The weather again deteriorated but our mobile Ground control units had moved up behind the Armies and were able to give directions although, in nearly all cases, the aircraft were returning friendlies. These patrols continued until 20th October.

The Germans put up stronger resistance and managed to hold onto Walcheren and the Hague which were out of range for the V.1.s. so it looks as though we will be called on to do intruder work again. Quite a lot of flying time was wasted by operating from Coltishall so it was decided that we should move to Castle Camps with effect from the end of the month. This was a newly built runway with long hard runways but for the Officer's mess they had taken over an old Mansion called Walterns Park and it was too far from our bungalow in Horning for us to live out.

This was a great disappointment as we had enjoyed our life there and Marie had found a Kindergarten school for Yvette. I had to stay in the mess for a while but then Marie came down and found a small cottage at Great Chesterford where we moved early in November and I was able to continue living out.

The Germans have still not abandoned their V.1. operations and in fact have discovered that not only can they launch them from the back of their old Heinkel 111 bombers but also that they can be flown over the sea at 200 feet at night by using a specially made radio altimeter. The plan was that these planes could be flown out from bases on the Dutch coast and launch their bombs from positions near the mouth of the Thames where they could easily reach London. At this height they could not be detected by our Radar Stations.

The boffins had also perfected a Radio altimeter and within a fortnight we had them fitted to our Mosquitos. These would give accurate readings from 500 feet down to sea level and they also had red and green lights. The green light came on above 200 feet and the red below 100 feet. The idea was that we should patrol at 1000 feet at positions about ten miles off the mouth of the Thames and, if we saw the launching flashes, to get down to 200 feet on the radio altimeter where our operators would scan the area looking for the Heinkels. The Mk X Radar was ideal for this as the sea reflections were helpful.

148

1, 2, 5 and 6 November: We did these patrols but the flashes we saw were very far away and Charlie could not get any contacts because the weather was too bad.

10 November: It was a better night and Bawdsey, our ground control station, had positioned us on a patrol line about twenty five mile east of the Thames just after midnight. After a while we saw flashes and got down to 200 feet where Charlie immediately picked up two contacts. We chased the nearest one and finally got close to it at a position thirty miles from the Hague. The problem was that we were now in his slip stream which was throwing us up and down at least fifty feet. It was also a very windy night and it was disturbing to see the red light flashing on and off. After a while, I saw his exhaust pipes and fired at 200 feet. One engine caught fire and almost immediately the Heinkel hit the sea and burst into flames. It was then that I saw we were only 20 to 30 feet above a very rough sea.

13, 19, 24 November: We carried out further patrols off the Thames without seeing any further flashes or enemy activity. It therefore seemed that the flying bombs, buzz bombs or doodlebugs, as they were generally known, had now finally finished.

Unfortunately, this was not to be the end of the bombing problems for London. Hitler had spent a great deal of money at Penemunde near Lubeck developing rockets and these were now to be fired from areas near the Hague. These rockets weighed about twelve tons and carried a one ton war head. Most of these fell wide of London but of the 1,300 that were fired, approximately 500 fell on London killing about 2,700 people and seriously injuring 6,500. The war head was much the same as the V.1.s but, as they hit the ground at such a high speed, they left enormous craters. Also there was no sound until they hit their target whereas people had got used to dropping flat when the buzz bomb motor stopped. These weapons were known as V.2.s.

There seemed to be nothing that Fighter command could do about these but Bomber command carried out mass raids on Penemunde. Probably their most effective action was the bombing of the huge caves that French intelligence reported were being used to store the V.2.s. They had once been used by mushroom growers but heavy bomber raids destroyed them and buried 600 bombs that were never recovered by the Germans.

The American Super Fortresses continued the daylight attacks on Peenemunde and the RAF bombers attacked all known factories that were making rocket components. Unfortunately, it was seven months before the Army could over-run these launching sites in the Hague.

We had a very quiet time in December as no further patrols were required and it was mainly spent in practice interceptions and gunnery exercises to keep our hands in. Christmas came and we were able to get leave to go to Chester and Leeds for a few days.

1 January: I was back on the Squadron and we were informed that we would be co-operating with Bomber Command and would be required to attend their briefing sessions. These were very large meetings with representatives from many Squadrons and plans were made for deceiving the Germans about where the raids were going to be. One device was called Window which entailed a few bombers dropping streams of silver paper of a length that would appear on enemy Radar, creating the impression of a massive raid.

Our role was to patrol the German night fighter aerodromes or areas between the fighters and the raid to try to pick up contacts and pursue the fighters. However, there were so many allied aircraft that most chases turned out to be friendlies. One disturbing moment was when we accidentally flew through one of our own bomber streams and although it was a non moon night we actually saw four bombers pass above and below us. The risk of collision was very high.

At the beginning of February, Marie's sister married an American officer, John Lowrey, and they had their honeymoon in London. We arranged to go down and see them for an evening and they were rather sad because John had to leave the next day to join his unit at Lille. This entailed two days travelling including the sea crossing. Most nights I was having to carry out night flying tests and I rather rashly suggested that if he could get to Castle Camps on the 7th I would drop him off at Lille during my flying test. Unfortunately, when we got there a thick snow storm made it difficult to find the base. When we finally did, I quickly dropped John off and taxied back to take off. The watch office obviously thought it was not safe to do so and flashed red lights at me. I had to ignore this in spite of red flares being fired as I had to be back at Castle Camps for night duty. Fortunately, I heard nothing more about the incident.

17 and 21 January: We carried out intruder patrols near the River Emms to Hamm and on 1st February to Dusseldorf but at no time did we get any contacts to follow up.

2 February: We did a four hour Bomber support patrol near Berlin but the one contact we had turned out to be a Mosquito path finder. It seems that the Luftwaffe now has very serious problems getting planes into the air and there is also an acute petrol shortage in the country.

3 February: I had a very pleasant surprise. I was notified that I had been awarded a bar to my D.F.C. and Charlie had also received the same which called for special drinks in the mess.

10 February: We had a seven day leave and went to Chester, Leeds and Scarborough, where father had recently retired. Now that Cardigan Press was going to survive the war, my uncle decided he wanted to come back and run it and father decided to let him take over. Our house at Horsforth was also rather a worry as Mr Prior, the builder, wanted payment for it. At the beginning of the war the Building Society had backed out of making a loan. People called into the services had protection so Mr Prior could not reclaim the house. We had been paying him interest on the money but now he wanted payment.

For this reason, we went to Leeds to see the married couple that had been renting it from us and they were most upset that we may want it back and even offered to buy it from us. When we went to Scarborough my father suggested that we rented a flat there for Marie and the family to settle in until I could get myself demobilised. The couple in our house offered us double the original price which was the current value of similar properties so we accepted their offer, paid off Mr Prior and put £1,000 in the bank.

When we returned to the Squadron, I still had to attend the Bomber briefings. We continued the bomber support intruder patrols although resistance to the advancing army was dissolving very fast. It seemed that Hitler was determined to make a last stand in Berlin. It was obvious that all the land the Russians had conquered would not be given up again after peace was declared. It therefore became a race for our Armies to occupy as much land as possible before the Russians.

21 February: We had a four hour patrol round eastern German airfields at Alhorn and Varrelbusch but no aircraft took off. We did a similar patrol to a large German airbase called Twente the next day but still no sign of enemy aircraft.

I now heard from my mother that they had found a flat in West Street which they thought would do for Marie until I was demobilised so we decided to take it and move out of the house at Great Chesterford.

27 March: I got leave and moved Marie with the girls and Edna to Scarborough. When I returned I lived in the mess at Waltens Park and kept Pookie with me. He was a very faithful and intelligent dog and slept under my bed at the mess. When I went up to Flights, he would lay next to my chair in the Flight Office and when I went off on patrols I would give him a pat and he would wait for an hour or two. He would then go and sit next to a WAAF driver in the transport who took air crew back and forth to the mess and she would take him back on the next trip. After this he would go to the kitchens where the WAAF cooks would feed him and finally to my bedroom to sleep until I returned. Pookie became very popular with all the Squadron.

Throughout the month of March, our nights were spent doing Bomber support flights or long intruder patrols round the German airfields but although we had many contacts and interceptions they all proved to be friendly.

153

4 and 8 April: We did our last two intruder patrols which were of long duration as they were near Berlin. Marx aerodrome was lit up for twenty minutes but no planes took off. On the 8th we spent five hours patrolling Neuroppin and Lieben Walde which had been very busy Luftwafffe stations but there was no sign of life so it seemed that it was all over. We flew for five or six hours in April but they were all practice interceptions to keep our hands in and for training of mobile G.C.I. stations.

22 April: Hitler tried to make a last stand in Berlin but most of his Generals had now deserted him.

29 April: Hitler finally committed suicide in his bunker. The Italian people had at last got their hands on Mussolini and after dismembering his body, they hung it up by the feet after dragging it through Rome at the end of a rope. So this was the inglorious end of the two great dictators who had threatened the world five years earlier.

Unfortunately, the Army advance had not got as far as Berlin and a large area to the west of the city was occupied by Russians. They clearly had no intention of leaving even though the Allies had landed and taken over the surrounding airfields. After Hitler's death Berlin was divided into American, British, French and Russian sectors which remained for many years to come.

It was a relief to have survived this terrible war but the worry now was Japan. It was clear that an all out effort would have to be made to finish them off and there was a strong possibility that our Squadron would be posted to the far east to take part in this effort. The Japanese were not the sort of people to surrender and they had many suicide pilots who believed that, if they were killed in action, they would get a glorious reception from their ancestors in the next world. It would obviously be highly dangerous to go into combat against this mentality.

1 May: I had by now been advised that I was to be presented with my decorations by the King so we arranged for Marie to come down today so that she could spend a couple nights in London. A reasonable number of visitors were allowed in the grounds of Buckingham Palace but only two next of kin were allowed into the Hall to see the presentation. Marie and Father came in. Mother, Ruth and Pat waited in the grounds. Charlie was also collecting his decoration and his parents and sister were there.

All the people to be decorated were ushered into a large reception Hall and instructed by some rather effeminate young men as to what they had to do. It appeared the King would be standing in the centre of a stage. We were to line up and walk slowly in front of him when our turn came, then turn left, salute, take a step backwards, bow and then step forward. The King would then pick up the medal from a cushion held by his aide and place it on a hook which had already been attached to our uniforms. He may ask a question, we would then salute, turn smartly to the right and march off, whereupon another aide at the end would snatch the medal from our chests, place it in a box and push it into our hands

This all sounded simple enough but it was surprising that a number of men who had shown courage in battle were very nervous. There were several who forgot to step back and the King had to dodge out of the way when they bowed. In the reception hall before we went in there was a toilet which amused the chaps as it was marked 'Crapper.' Apparently the palace installed one of the first water closets in the last century and the French designer was Mr Thomas Crapper, hence the expression which at the time was vulgar although not in the Victorian period. After the event, we all had lunch at a good Hotel before returning home.

For the rest of May we were carrying out training exercises and taking senior people over the bombed areas of Germany to see the damage to the Cities. At this time, the concentration camps had been overrun and the Cinemas and papers were showing the horrors of Belsen and Dachau. The relieving forces could only give them food and make the German people in the surrounding area go in, clean them up and wash the poor people that had survived. At this time too, the prisoners of war camps had been released and a friend that I had joined up with returned home. He was Henry Heaton. We had trained together but he had opted for Bombers and had been shot down in a Wellington on his fourth mission. He had survived with a leg injury but had spent four years in prison.

He telephoned me in July at Castle Camps and said he would like to fly again before he was demobbed. I spoke to Willum Hoy and he said to invite him for a few days to stay at the mess. This I did and Henry seemed his old self and joined in well with conversations over dinner. Over the next day or two I took him up in our Tiger Moth and an Oxford both of which were dual control and let him fly and land them. He had not lost the touch. I also took him up in a Mosquito. When I saw him off I thought he was no worse for his imprisonment but over the next year he developed an introverted nervous problem which interfered with his work. He was a Director of the family firm, Heaton clothiers, but he had to resign because his nerves became so bad that he couldn't leave his house. The problem did not improve in the rest of his short life.

July was spent on training exercises and camera gun practices. Early August was the same and then on the 6th August it was announced that the Atom bomb had been dropped on the city of Hiroshima in Japan, causing the destruction of almost the whole of it. The Japanese would still not surrender even though they were threatened with a second bomb if they refused. In the event, a second bomb had to be dropped on Nagasaki resulting again in total destruction and enormous loss of life. After this the Emperor bowed to the inevitable and accepted defeat.

Our training exercises continued into September when the anniversary of the Battle of Britain came round. I was told I had to lead a small formation of Mosquitos in a big Fly Past of different Squadrons over London. This was organised by Douglas Bader, the famous legless ace from the Battle of Britain. I had not met him before and he had been in prison for two years. He was the most energetic man and had tried to escape so many times that the Germans decided to take his artificial legs away.

In October Willum Hoy said that I had to take "A" Flight to Lubeck near the Baltic to carry out exercises there. The Air base was a pre-war German one and had escaped the war almost untouched. The H.Q. buildings and Officer's mess were like a first class hotel and many types of German aircraft were parked round the perimeter all with empty tanks. I found it most interesting to be able to climb into the cockpits of Heinkels, Junkers and Messerschmitts of all types and closely examine these machines which we had been pursuing for the last five years.

We carried out the required exercises for the next fortnight and were able to fly to Copenhagen for two nights. The shops here were still well stocked with goods, not at all like England where everything is very basic. I was able to buy a tea service with a design for Marie as you could only buy white pottery at home. I also bought two dolls for the girls with eyes that moved, unheard of in the U.K.

19 October: The Flight Sergeant informed me that the fitters were short of some small parts to service the planes. I said that if he would give me a list I would fly to Castle Camps and bring them back. When I arrived in England, William told me that my Demobilisation papers had come through and that he would send someone else with the parts. I said my farewells and went to London to get final clearance and a demob suit, which was nearly as bad as the first uniform I had received at Cardington.

I was soon back at home with Marie, a marvellous feeling of warm security, a loving wife and two beautiful children. I went back to Cardigan Press for about three weeks but under my uncle's rule it seemed impossible. Also at best I would have to share my future with two cousins. These were not my sort of people. Whilst in Scarborough I saw an opportunity to start a small Photogravure business and I set this up with my gratuity and the £1,000 we had made out of the house. But that is another story.

PHOTOGRAPHS

Officers and Aircrew of No. 255 Squadron circa 16th July 1942

Squadron 255 Dinner

When the mainspring of their gramophone breaks Douglas Greaves and Fred Mitten Robbins, his tail-end Charlie, wonder what Montgomery would do as, with the help of some pendulums, they devise a way to play records on a makeshift gramophone.

Douglas Greaves and Fred Mitten Robbins, his tail-end
Charlie in North Africa.

Flying buddies: Doug Greaves with wartime colleague
Charlie Robbins.

Douglas and Phil Kendall outside Buckingham Palace after being awarded the DFC and Bar

Douglas, his wife Marion and Fred Robbins outside
Buckingham Palace after the award ceremony

Men and Machine: Fred Robbins and Douglas Greaves with their Second World War aircraft.

A Bristol Beaufighter flown by Douglas and Fred Robbins.

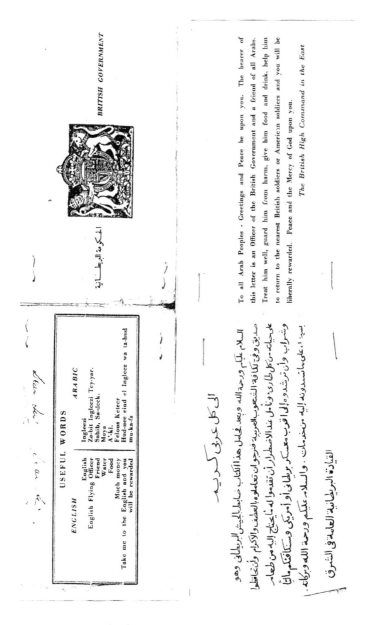

Help for 'Downed' Air Crew.

Printed in Great Britain
by Amazon

73673300R00102